Art Center College of Design
Library
1700 Lida Street
Pasadena, Calif. 91103

**R**      **E**

ART CENTER COLLEGE OF DESIGN

SPEC.
741.60922
N354
A2
2003
c.2

Edited by Robert Klanten
Published by Die Gestalten Verlag, Berlin

Printed by Juette-Messedruck, Leipzig
Made in Europe

Bibliographic information published by
Die Deutsche Bibliothek

Die Deutsche Bibliothek lists this publication in the
Deutsche Nationalbibliografie; detailed bibliographic
data is available in the Internet at http://dnb.ddb.de.

© dgv - Die Gestalten Verlag, Berlin 2003
ISBN 3-931126-73-0

All rights reserved. No part of this publication
may be reproduced or transmitted in any form
or by any means, electronic or mechanical,
including photocopy or any storage and retrieval
system, without permission in writing from the
publisher.

For your local dgv distributor please check
www.die-gestalten.de

Respect copyright, encourage creativity.

Neasden Control Centre was formed by visual agents Stephen Smith and Marcus Diamond. They work in all forms of graphic communication and are based in London, UK.

For more information:

http://www.neasdencontrolcentre.com
info@neasdencontrolcentre.com

All Artwork: Neasden Control Centre Ltd

Stephen Smith, Marcus Diamond, Ross Holden, Matt Ward

Art Direction: Smith and Diamond

Neasden Control Centre would like to thank everyone they know and love.

| | |
|---|---|
| WD | _WORDS |
| SK | _SKETCHBOOKS |
| DR | _DRAW |
| PA | _PAINT |
| DS | _DESIGN |
| OB | _OBSCURE |
| ARC | _ARCHITECTURE |
| FO | _FOUND OBJECTS |
| CO | _3D |
| E | _EDITIONS |
| MU | _MUSIC |
| D | _DARK |

WD

TITLE: POLEMIA

WORD COUNT: 2008

Art Center College of Design
Library
1700 Lida Street
Pasadena, Calif. 91103

## _ POLEMIA

The day before the day after next, yesterday came and went. I'd been listening to the Shaving Cuts. Were they deep? Part one and part four maybe but what about the other parts? I guess as a two bit piece they felt they were good enough not to be just hiding down the side of the sofa. Don't forget to check in. They were supporting music made by the Big Jellied Men. No backbone you see as you've decided to cut a funny dot comedy into your face with only a pistachio and then you find your arm doesn't work and only drips gossip gristle until you make a chequered line around it. Be careful with the wrapping and refracting. Great guns or piss poor floating on a door under glass. Let the bully boy boos sink the Hawaii 501. Use his molars. All 2 of them. Nomadic sandwater. Better free spoonish reacted the Neolithic speak and speller. Metallic freudless. Cyclops was eating the cloud making machine. Printed mild matter. A floating tin shed next to the magic little man with a runaway pen in his bruised hand. Eat some soggy sliced bloody bread. Alpha 2 emerges as the sword swinger solo. Grinding chew bass with tongue and grooved. Replacing this with that. Bleep. Cash. Comma. Beep. Blot. Whirling. Spinning. The last thing I remember saying was dive Captain dive. It's weird how my head feels cold from the water. What I've written seems different since I was always asked to draw circles in 3D. What for? So eventually I did draw a circle on your back and with which finger did I touch it last? I'm fav / odds to evens as the going is good for the disc / horse jockey Alan.J.Leeback the younger who was dissecting some black circling one groove noisy vinyl through and above the approx operating time of 15-20 hours depending on freshness of batteries. Down down through the coiled black wires which didn't build Rome in a day, but are about 3 miles in circumference. 4 X 1.5 volt monosyllables in constant heavy stereo. We're transmitting from the ant antenna across every waterproof microwaved map in sight. Can you hear me? Spool size 3 inches. Can you see me? Mean tape size speed 3 per second sq. The lights are flashing 12 volt nonsense and not stopping. Red and yellow analogue steel gears fab I clicked as I lit the back bunsen burner. I'm going to hate that vacuum packed bridge. These run down technicalities are held together with gaffer on my sellotaped face. Record 1 of 101. This is the Knitted Mice with their latest 11" single: Blown Dynamo Blues. Play. Sound. Loudspeaker -3,5 ohm. Elliptical foiled finger pointing at the sky but my hair was still cut off. I thought about unplugging Frankenstein's monster equation. Perhaps that would stop the buzzing in my tiny shell-like. What were those bleeps? No matter for as long as I could see a piece of Albert's light I knew I'd be alright. That old noise geography eh? Spring finally became Summer. That's tough like the rest of the greased fringed cowboys who were being steamrolled into saltwater dust, all of which would be kept neatly in a foreign typed box. Fair enough. Sounds like I'm in a car boot sale and my lung capacity is nearly up. I'll close my small eyes and try and wake up when I know exactly where I am. Dark rusted streaks crossed my lids as the four circles turned a corner and I plotted Autumn so it felt like a disease that has no sound so who knows how it smells? In the Winter I bumped into Mr Claw the one wheeled crab who was wondering with which typeface to sit. Who is that person? I can't seem to make them out. On no account allow the pen to leave the paper while the extensions are running from the Wembley Twins; Twiggy and Al. You can see them now thanks to the lights from the northern circular. Here's the evidence: a stainless steel briefcase, a well, a single camera lens and a telephone made from masking tape. I think he also wrote a poem on the side of a bin whilst I was sat in row 1, seat 13B. Bleep and festering noise machine is extra. Enjoy your visit. Come in Mr Satum your time is up as current consumption which started out as a two-horse chariot race is nearly over. This radio is 200-100 medium wave at the motor, approx amplifying on 200m / 15ma. This is your final destination from him I mean her, I mean them. But who really does love the Invisibleman? And can I quote you on that? He's got an action like a rattlesnake looking for food in Dr Bears surgery whilst walking the plankton. And on day 8 God finally created ducks with wings, ankle hips and ember bags. Bang bang there's a promo Stamford so cheer up bedbox. How about them apples? Magic darts. Oh what's your number lads? Alright boss he's un fuego that Neville, Butt, Neville sister as it's what the chicks dig so lets swap sidebums. No I don't want a sister I want a monkey. 1234 I declare a thumb war so make yourself look like a big pencil and shorten your lead Mr Doberman. Rain poured more heavily now as Costa Del Zorro crept to the field line. Around him were peat bog cairns and at some point I don't know which I finally remembered the punch line to the joke, which reads as follows: if I don't go on before the juggler then I'm not going on at all. She murmured a gesture and stood up. The day was now darkening over and she felt that if she didn't go now she never would and so she took her chance, carefully moving into a large noisy crowd that was now heading eastwards. He was still laid on his back watching the clouds coming over and carried on talking at pace unaware but well aware of fairgrounds as a child. One was called Crows Fair, but how far and wide it travelled I don't know. He was cut off as the bloody battle raged on. Scissors. Where is my sword? On paper I demand you yield the siege of Bentley. Answer. They were all around us and the sound was deafening. Your injury meant we stayed here to gather ourselves. I bandaged your bloody hands and spoke fetch my horse Polemia. Prepare her in goldleaf. Now apply earth to your mouth. Replace arrowheads with useless words. Watch the clearlake then gather stones and tie this lock of hair to him. Wrap rope and goose fat around him then burn the body. Then scatter Palmers Field with poppy seeds. It was one hell of a scary visit, no doubt and as an indicator to the scale of terror involved they were only ever allowed to set up in the field next to the fire station. My favourite ride was the waltzers because rules were simple, if you wanted to go all out ride it with lots of girls and the operators will come and give them the extra pushes. Spinning at a high velocity. Focus. Working components. Thickly greased. Solid. Heavy. That was the Morecambe mousetrap. Are you listening? He stood and watched motionless the coloured whizzing lights and bells until it started to make him feel nauseous. He turned away clutching his kite and had a funny thought about what he wanted to be when he grew up which he was now. He enjoyed visiting the past and read every single word to avoid the photocopied ones. Inky fuzzy lines of black and grey. Outflank them down at the ship merchants dock and kick a butterfly two-stroke wind section Mingus or shoot old bass bins from the tin roof that holds our weightlessness exactly. Would I be able to hold my breath long enough to swim under the British Isles? For some reason he was able to gauge when the weather was about to change just like cows. Some strong pills had created an imbalance in his right ear which was now so sensitive he could detect the slightest change in pressure. Having a barometer for an inner ear and a copy of an old National Geographic as a wrist cam will surely stand you in good stead if you decide to become an astronaut. The one constant he definitely remembered was as a strong thirteen year-old breaking the school record for the javelin throw. It eventually landed in a Joseph Beuys painting. And unknown to him it still is. It's going to rain if you're freewheeling on your bike today thought her parents who were a happily married couple and had lived together for well over 12 years with nothing unusual but for the very fact of during 11 of them he hadn't spoke. One day returning from the Ant Museum he visited regularly once a year he calmly sat down and never spoke again. Months then years of nothing and nothing again to say. Not a pip. His wife had eventually learned to live with it, replacing her imagined words for his as now he was literally just part of the furniture. She used to hoover her husband daily using the A19 on the way up and the A6 on the way down. Hide those bloody ant maps as she called them when trapped on the canal tow path. Now they were just a huge collection of imagined places never visited, but extremely detailed. The shed was full steam ahead of them with intricate beautiful wooden boats each 2ft long in length from pier to pier estimated Eric Corrie. Springwell was a pike that scar felled it's way up the beck and round the Escher waterfalls. Kissing her Dad goodbye he passed her a folded envelope. On it was written just one word. She arrived back at the hotel and found her dog slightly ajar. She gently slipped silently onto the cold bare red tiled floor exhausted by the brief encounter on the 4 hour bus trip. Now she just had to sleep. She fell onto the bed and began to drift off immediately. "Go to sleep now" Bluebird and Owl said. This story you're about to read was found inside a mangled brown box, written as it was on some dusty carbon papers which had been washed up onto a beach on the North Eastern coastline. Due to the nature of the tides, lots of objectives end up here. One day I even found an entire lead suit. The label suggested it was Norwegian. I'd left my mullet in New York next to a ridiculous puffa beatbox crew and a signal lamp that could be spotted from where we sat next to the technical noise sound of space rockets and pentop robots scouting the international shooting unions 10 metre air rifle target. Texas Pete and the telephone babies were giving big comic cop banter to Smoky Joe from Mexico. I tell you it gives door stripping a new name. What about North pole dancing as a show? St George of Hamson was finding it increasingly difficult to magnetise the others while all the time Ray Mears was telling us he can light a fire anywhere. Bergerac can't investigate whilst on a ghost train on the fasttrack until the penny drops into the Neolithic site. Run suit run and imagine a torch so powerful it lights up space. Come and have a go because this daddies got fighting fizzy pop in his belly. Down at the Olympic Cafe I argued it's no more like jumping than sliding. What a din and vision from the reactors 1-7 because it's all trebuchets nowadays. Apparently the worlds tallest man lives in Neasden. 7ft 9 inches of pure luna soil. And remember in the grand scheme of things when shaving always cut off your mustache first just in case you pass away during the event and end up being buried with one. Night vessels must be anchored.

17.11.02

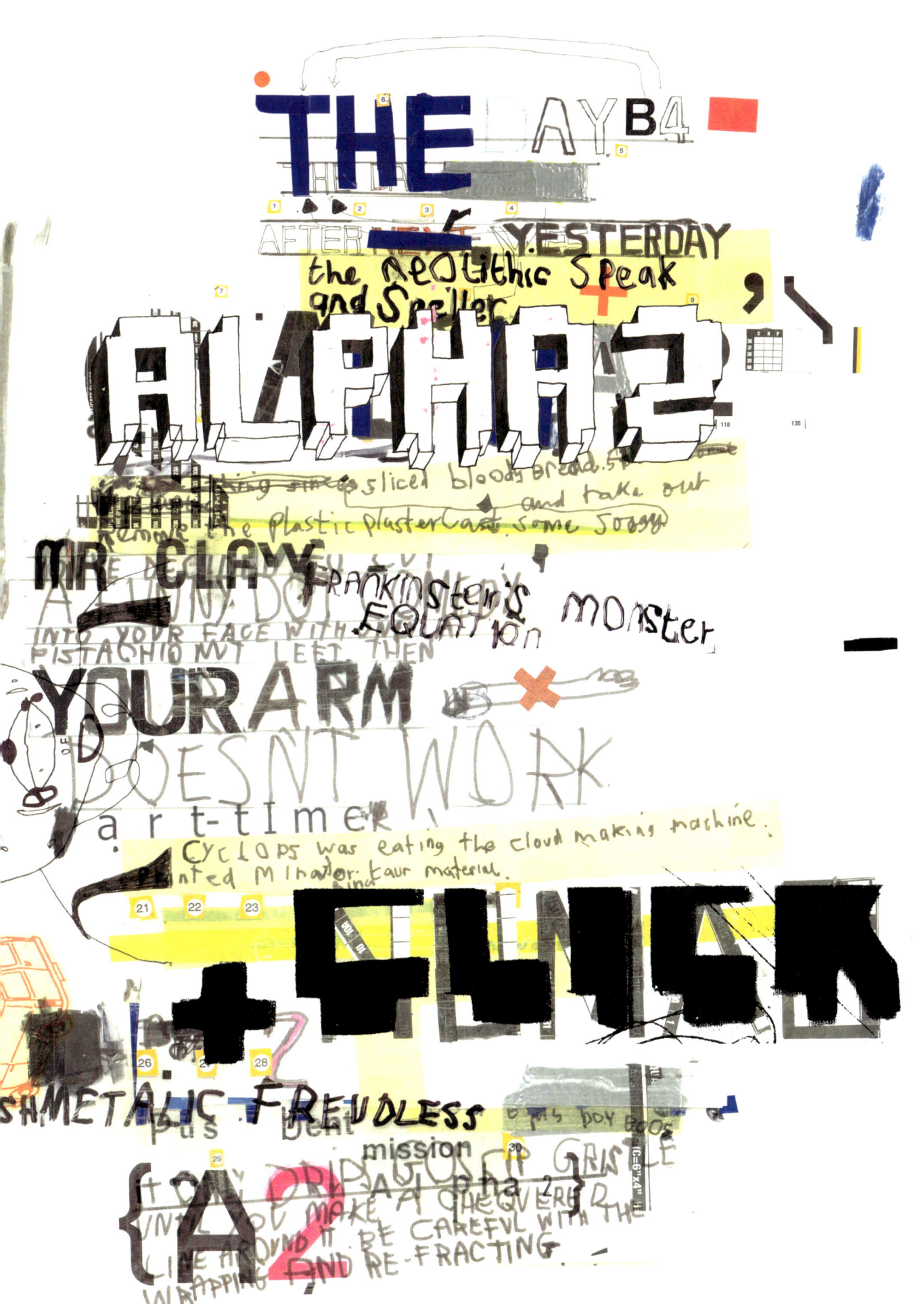

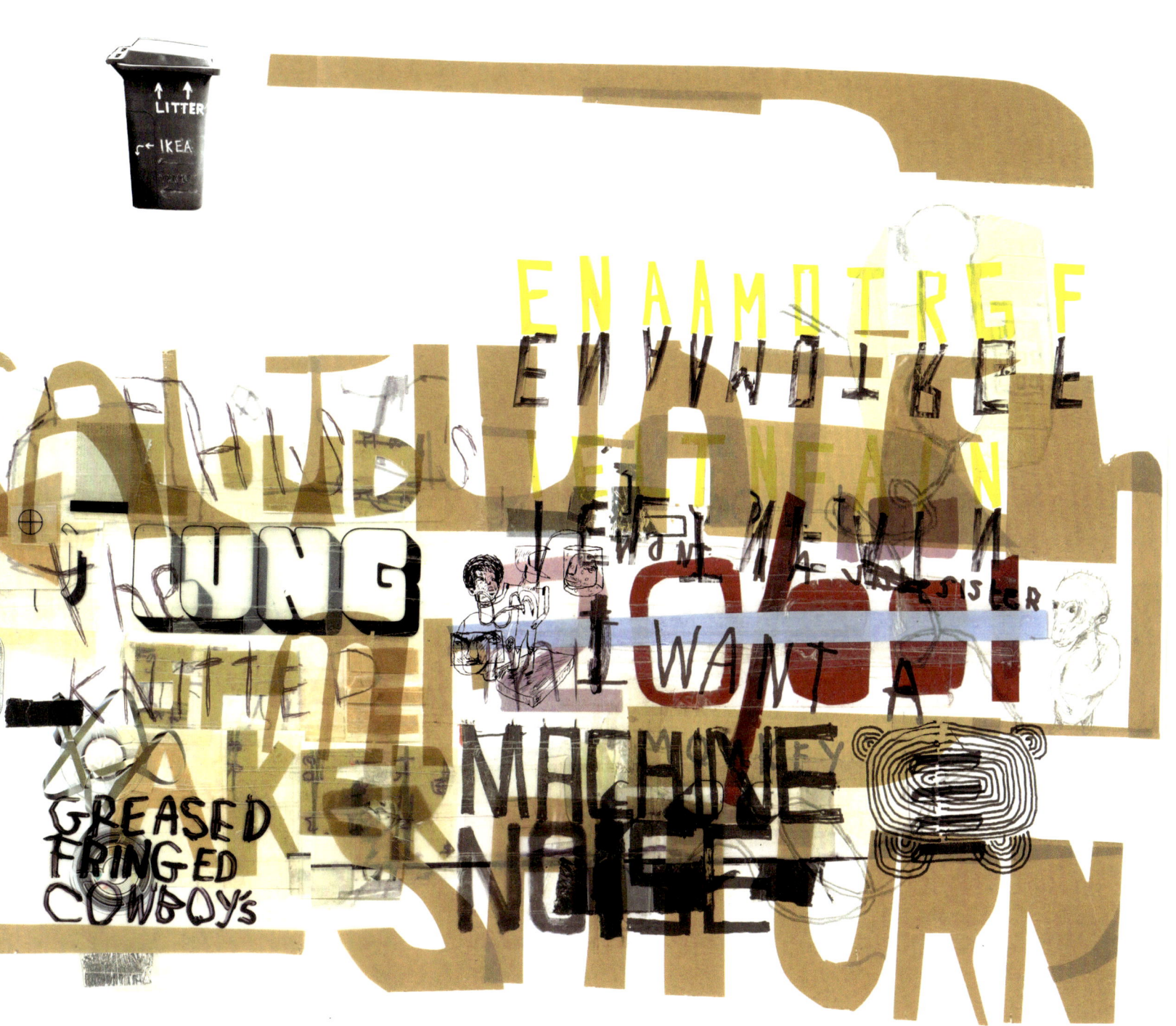

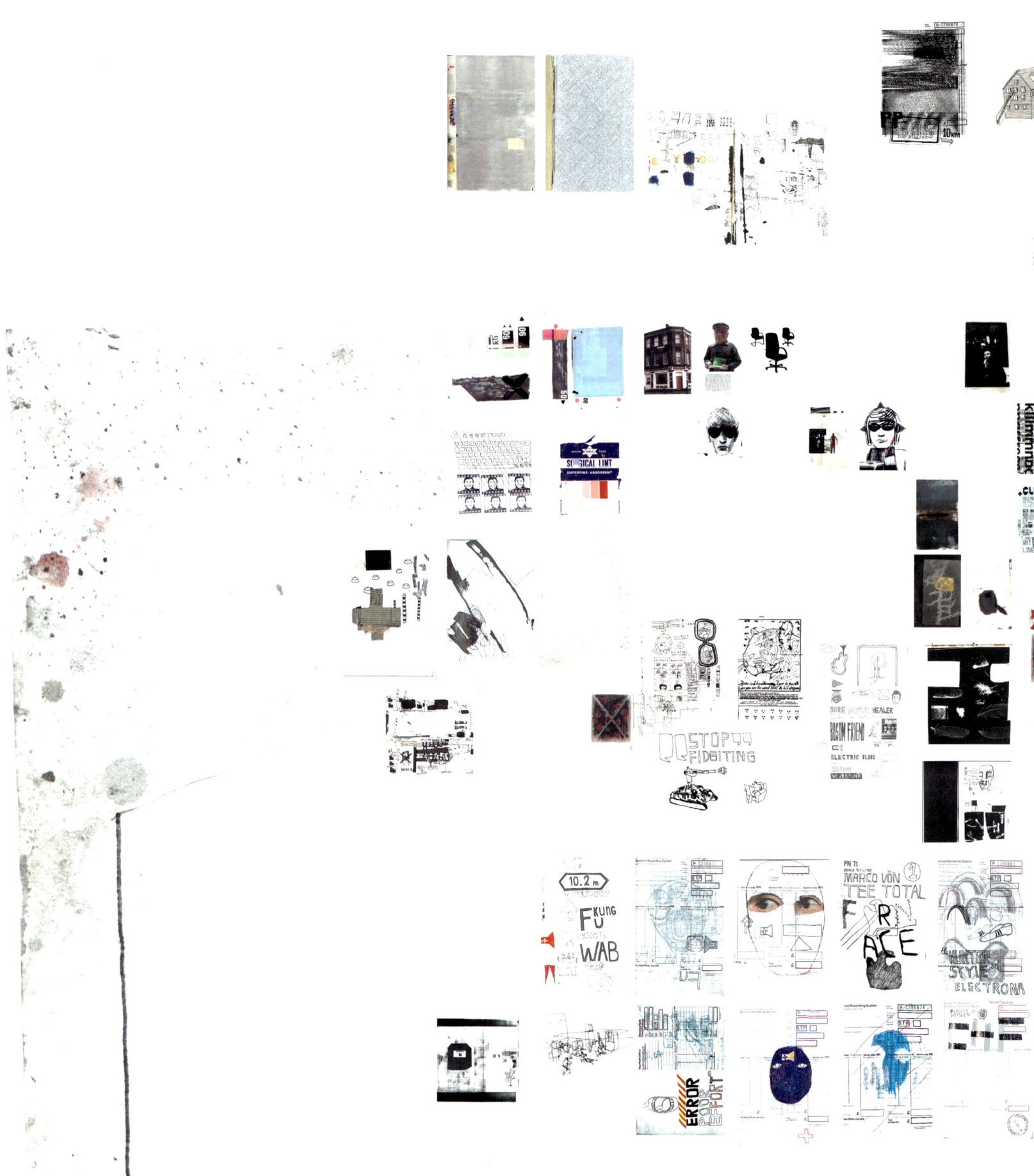

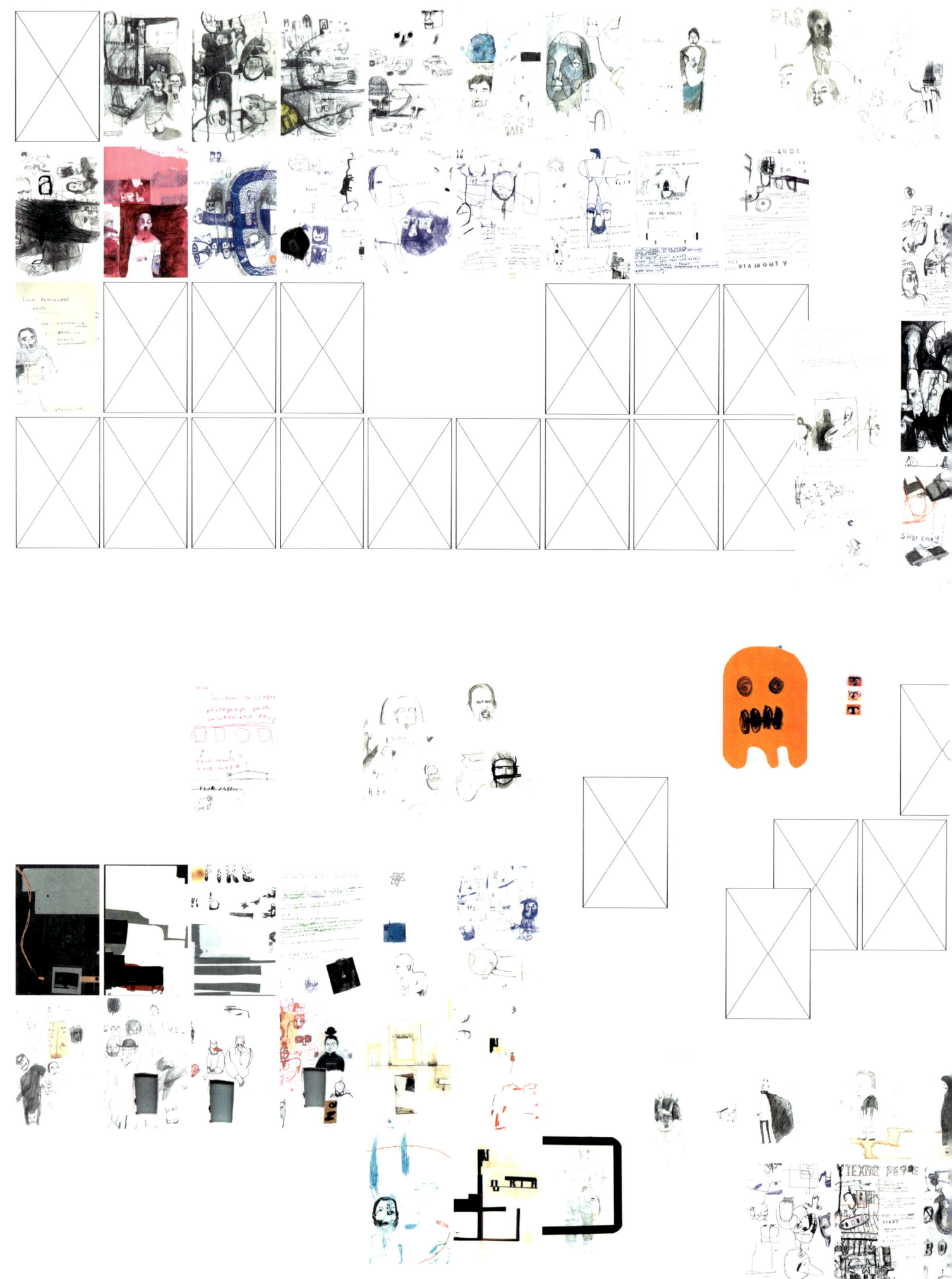

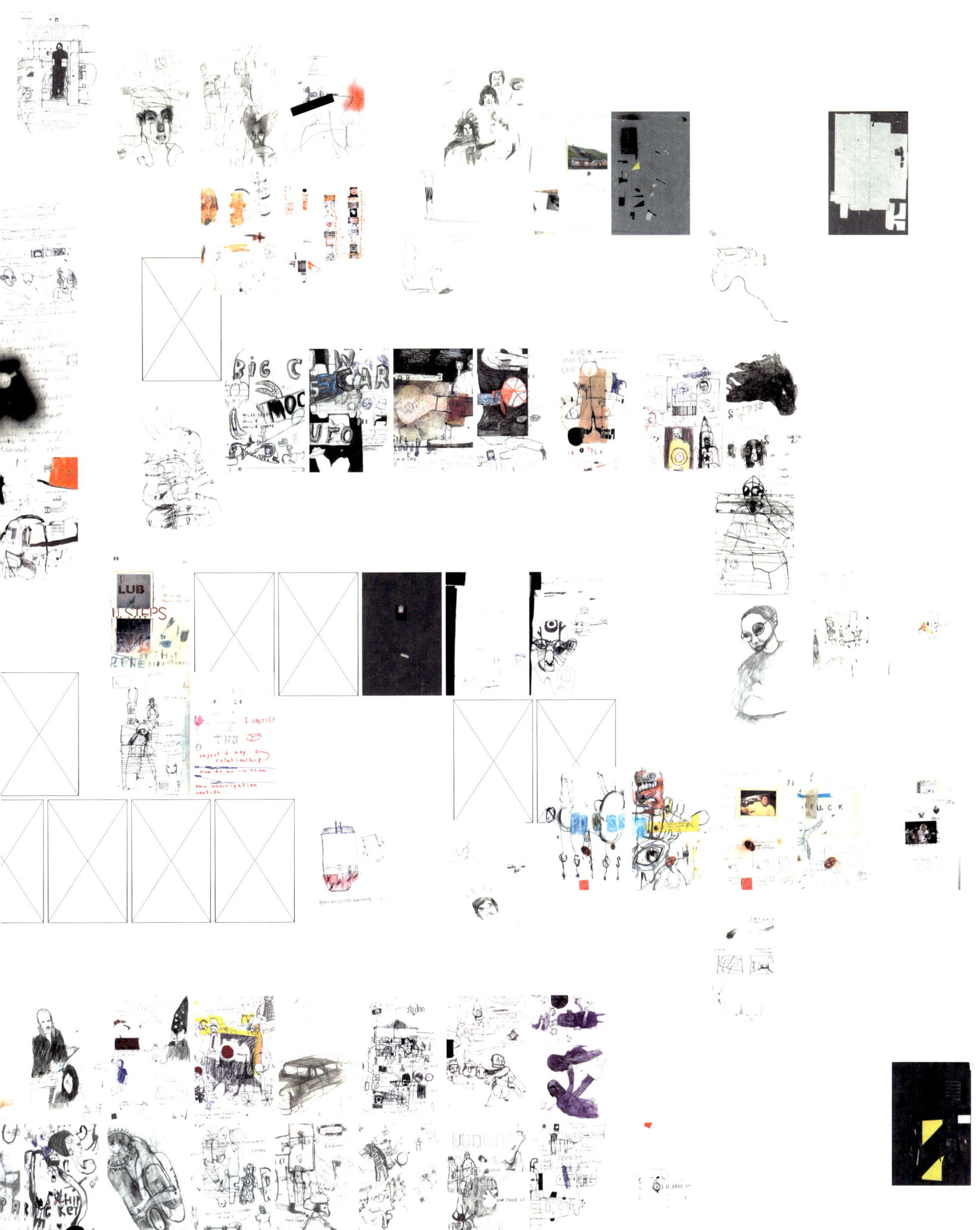

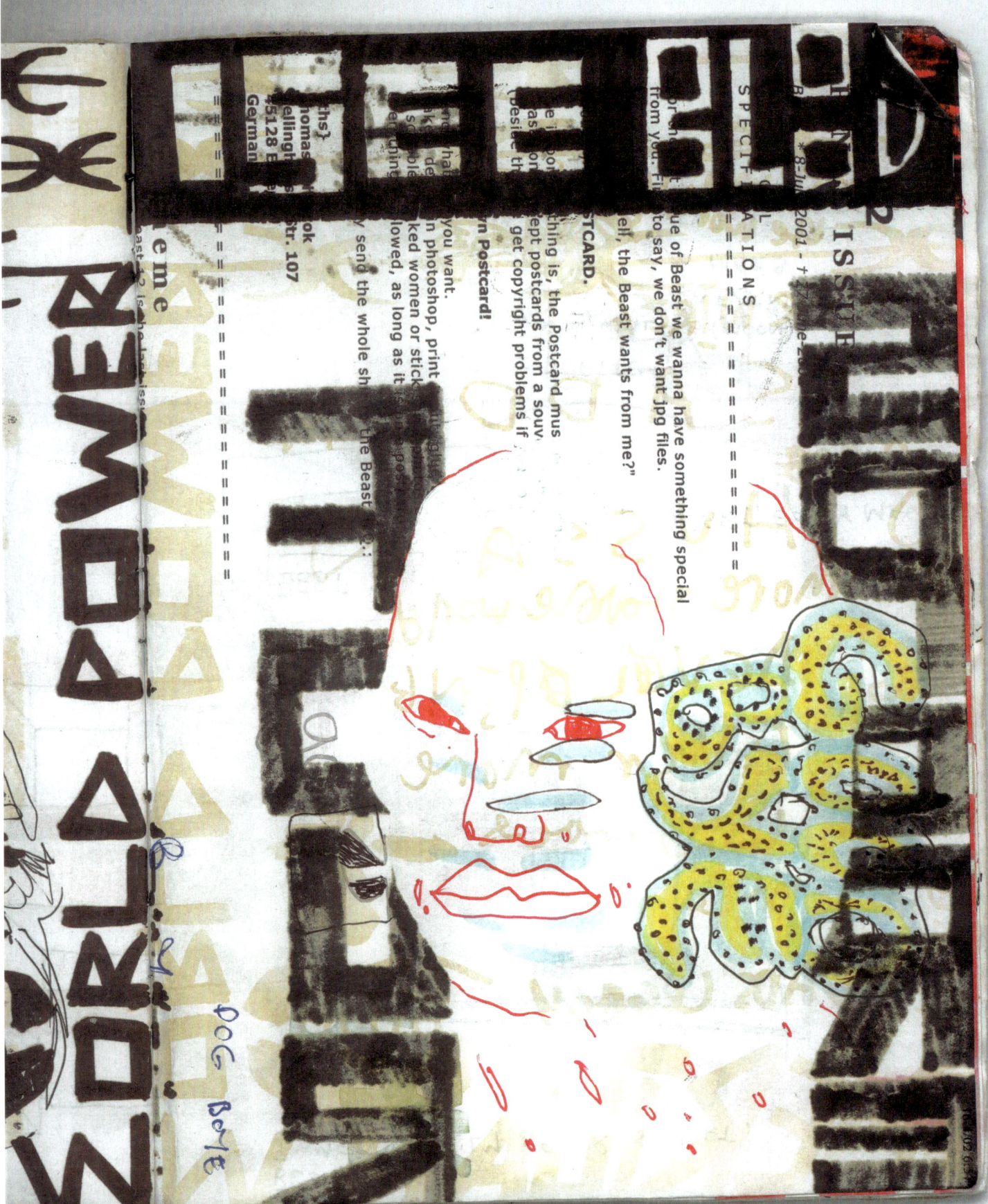

Kelly - 7 71 36 27
@zoom.co.uk

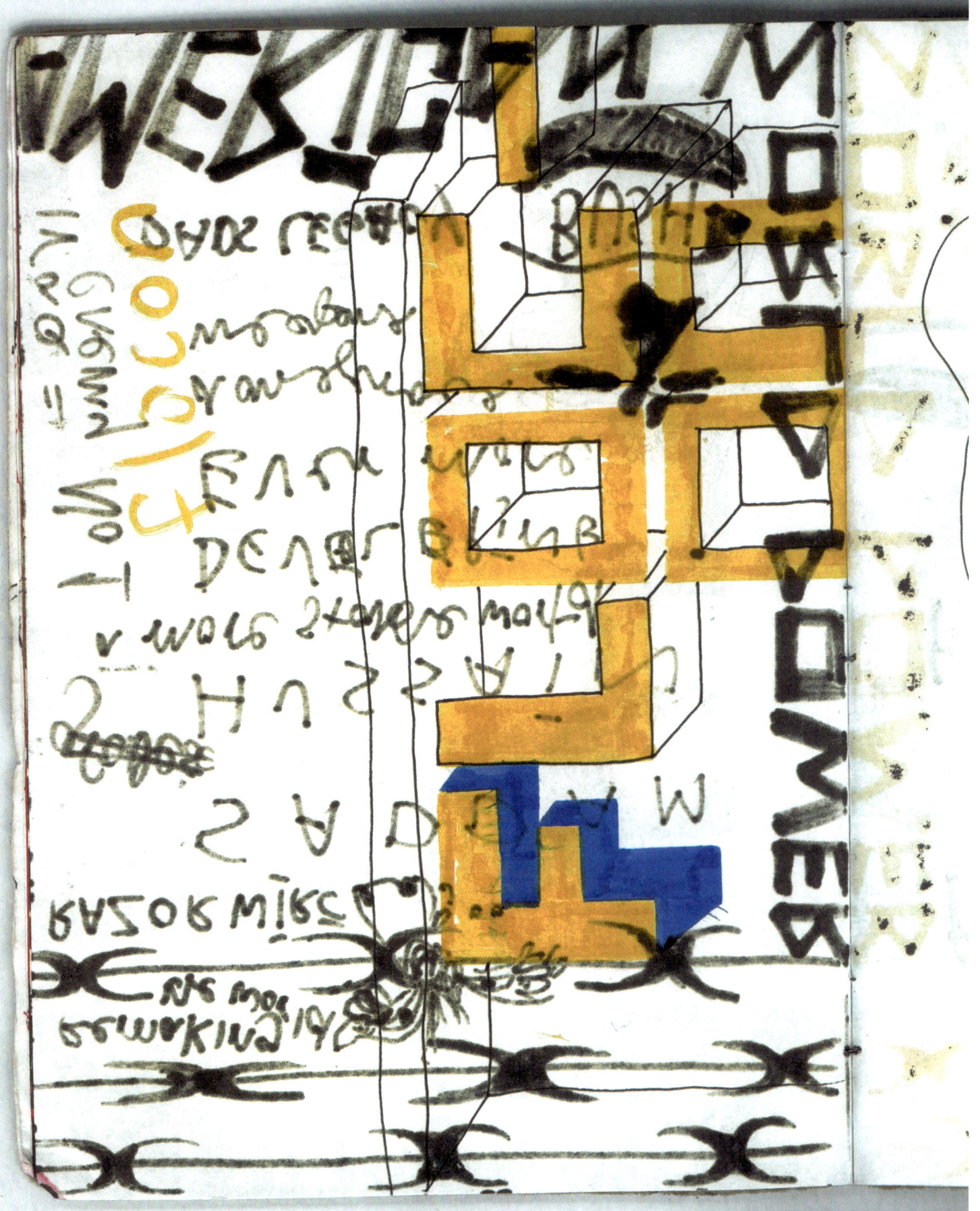

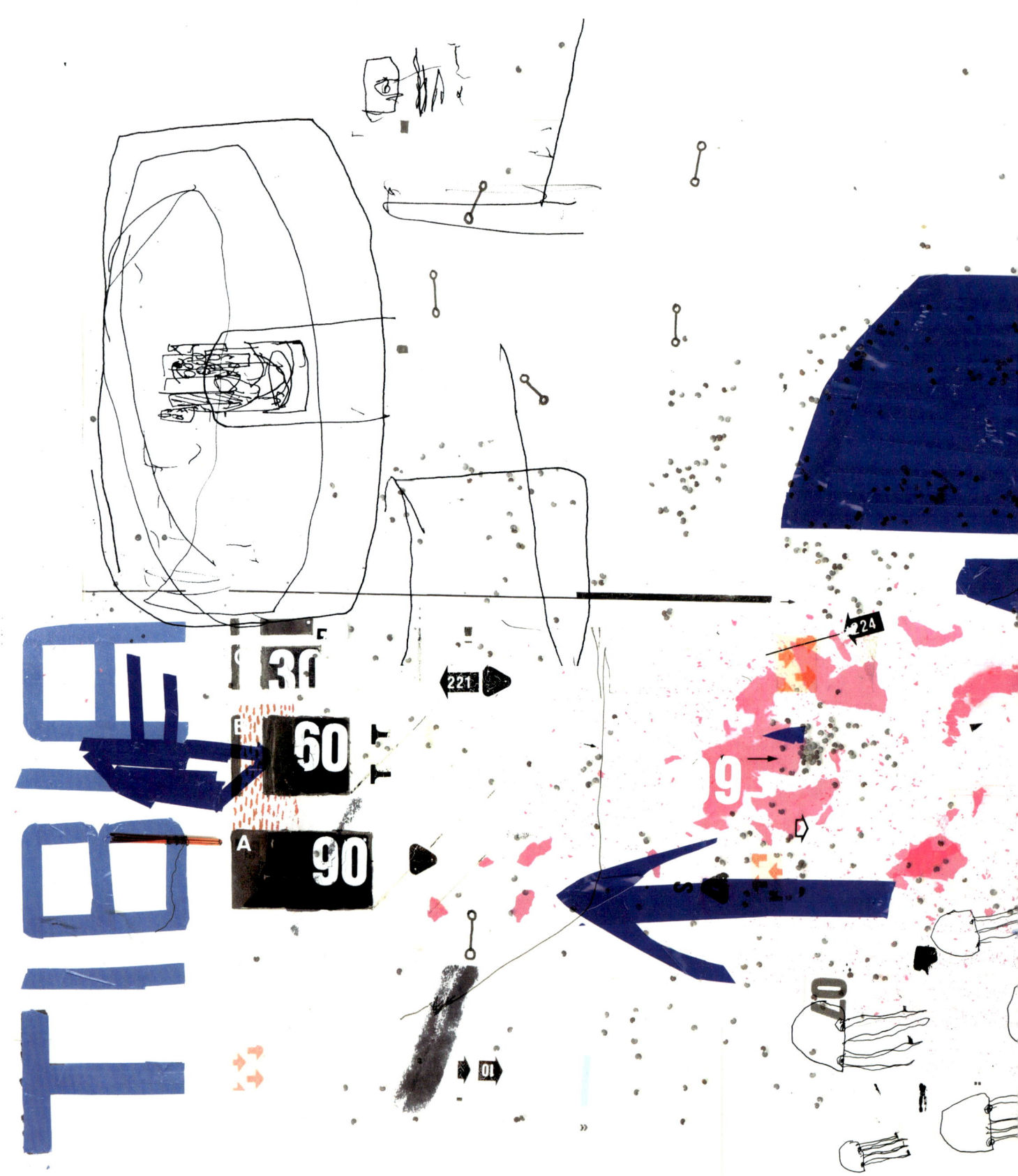

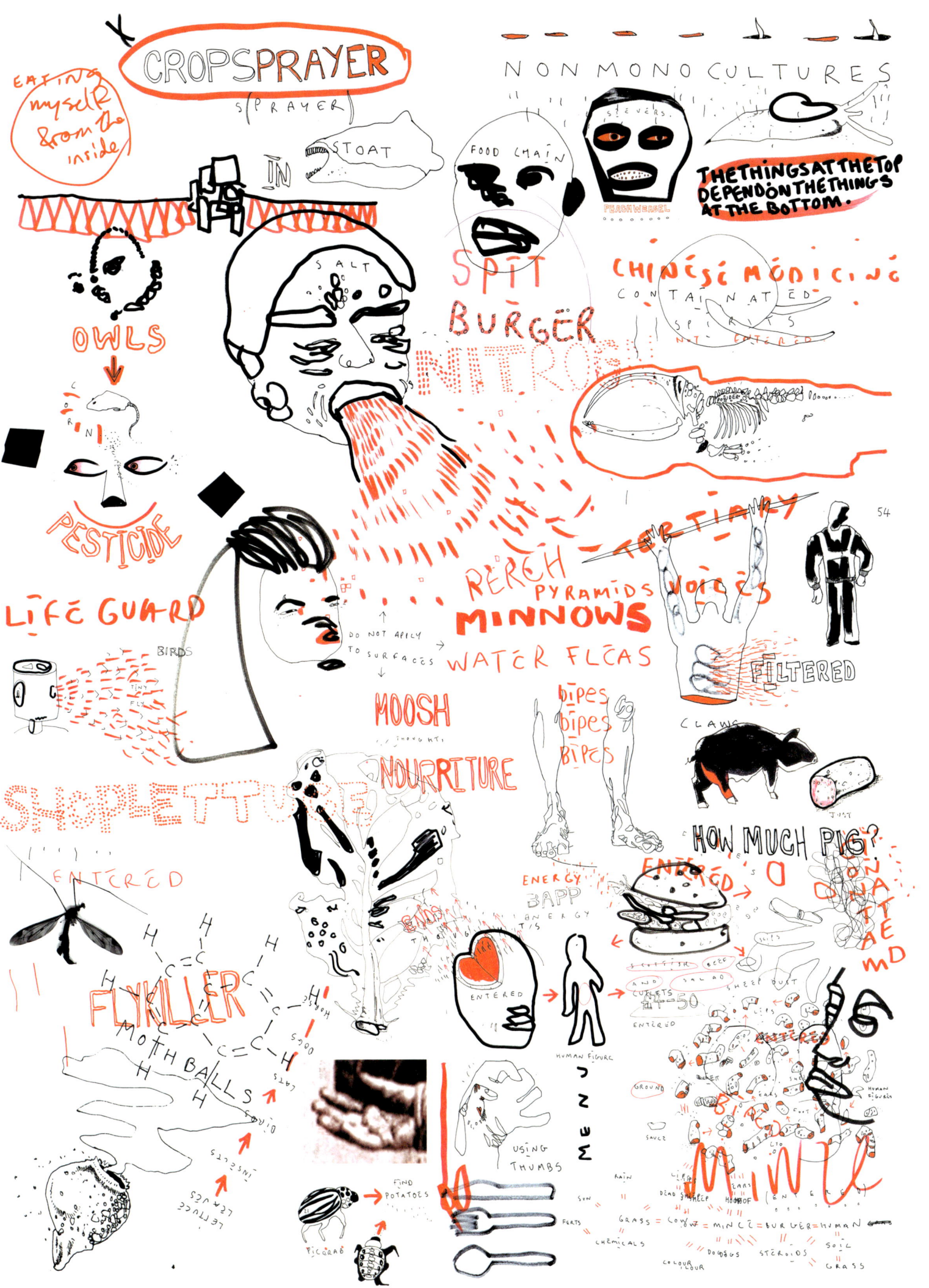

Art Center College of Design
Library
1700 Lida Street
Pasadena, Calif. 91103

1

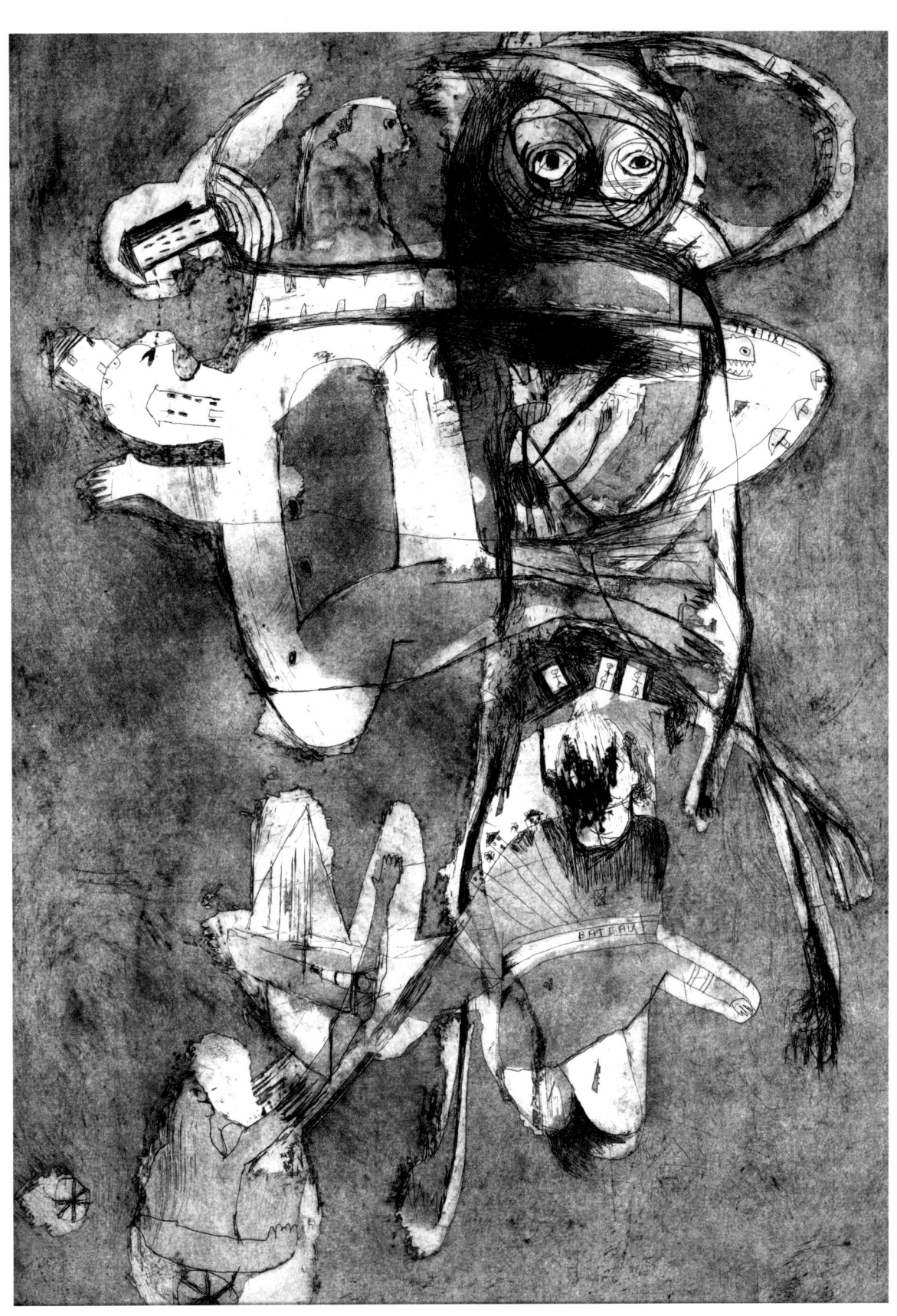

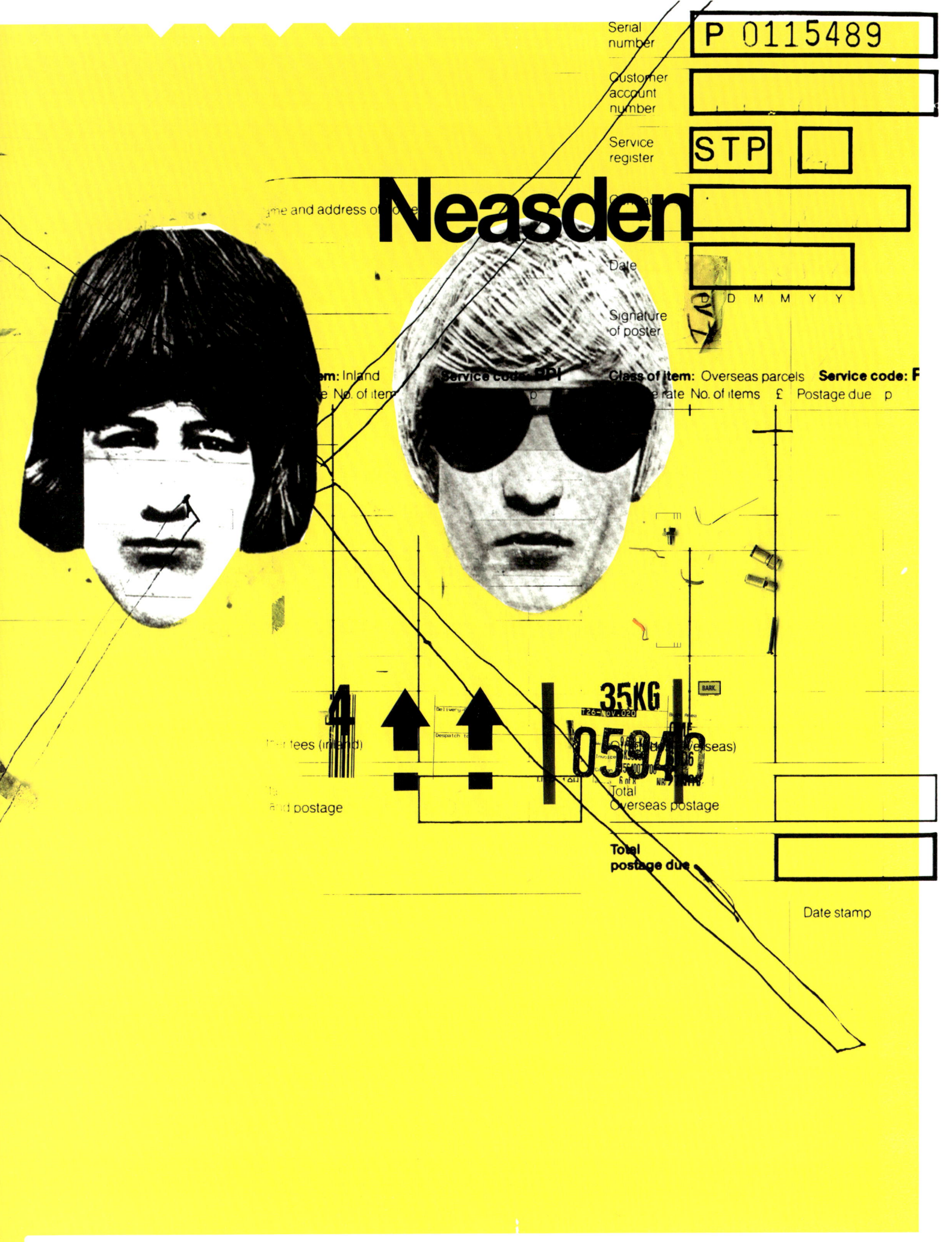

SHORT
YOUR L
MR D

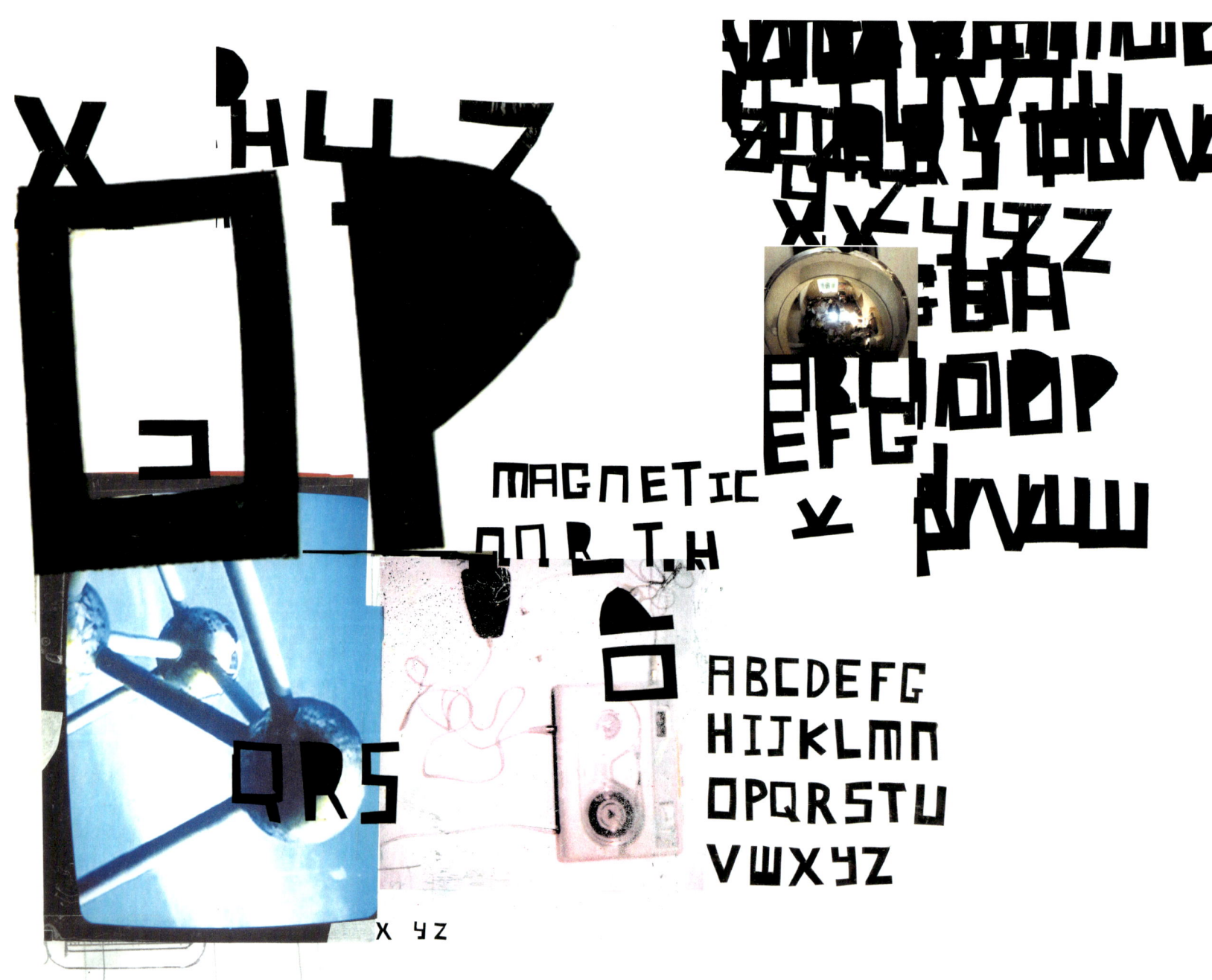

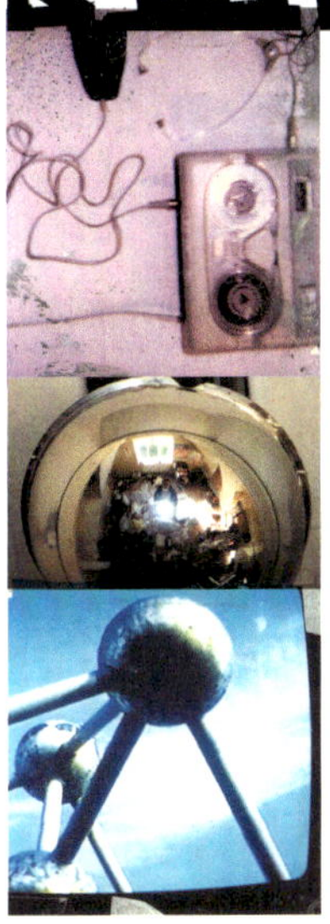

DS

TYPEFACE: THE GAFFER

ABCDEFGH
IJKLMNOP
QRSTUVW
X YZ

0123456789

#%^£@✦✦
[—?+=-[]..
*¶¶π:◨◧▫ ¨

Bring it on

ART DIRECTION: HTTP://WWW.O-6-N.CO.UK

# ASYLRECHT

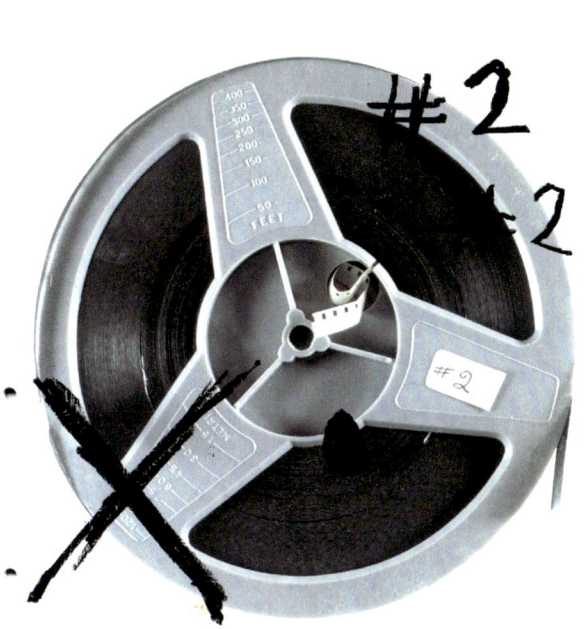
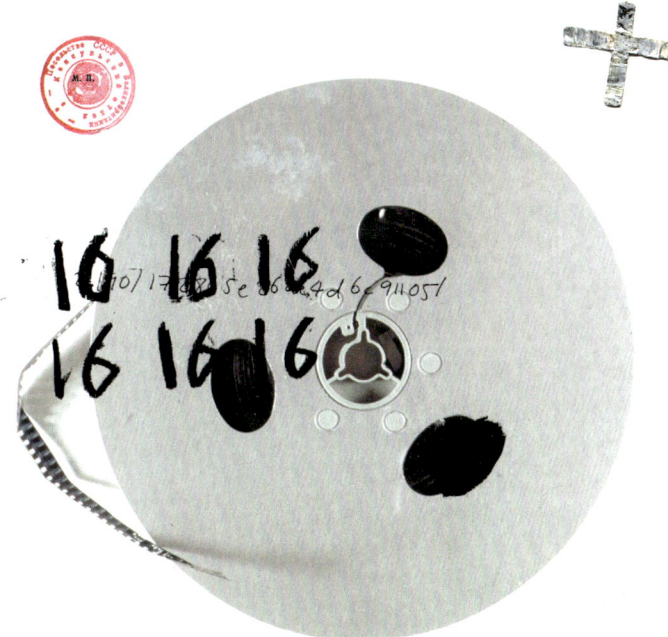
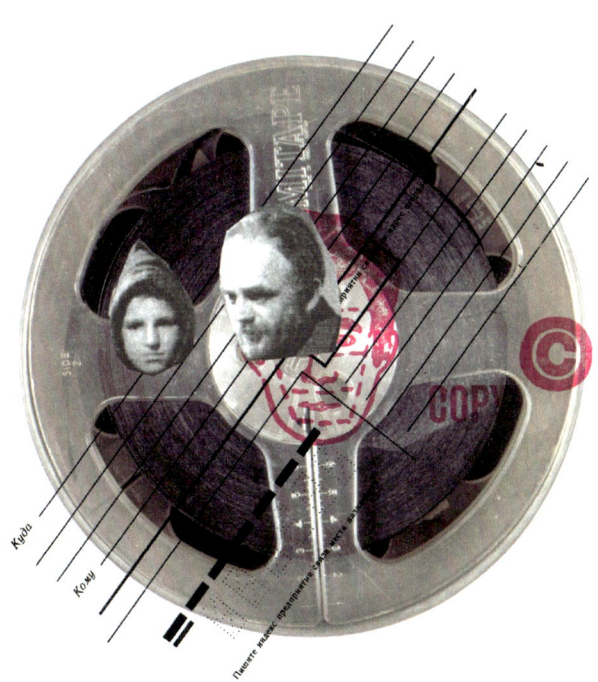

Warehouse Gallery
Brewery Arts Centre
Highgate
Kendal
Cumbria
LA9 4HE

Tel: 01539 722833 (admin)
01539 725133 (box office)
Fax: 01539 730257

admin@breweryarts.co.uk
http://www.breweryarts.co.uk

**"ASYLRECHT - THE RIGHT TO ASYLUM"**
PRODUCED BY ANOTHER SPACE

Featuring a section of the Berlin Wall (courtesy of the Yorkshire Sculpture Park) and **ASYLRECHT** - the censored documentary film of 1949 by Peter Shankland. Showing courtesy of the Bundesarchiv and the Shankland family.

# DOLLIS HILL

**74321 · 2 · CHASE ME · 610 YARDS · INSPECTION GOING GOOD TO SOFT IN PLACES · 8-676**

## TODAY'S RUNNER'S AND RIDERS: 3:45 PM

| | | | |
|---|---|---|---|
| WORM CAKES & Cº | Dr. BEAR FELTIPER 0487 | VOLT STORE IS HIGH | HOT ROD FLY RUN |
| NINE COLD PISS WAY | THE GUINEA JAW | TIN CAT RUTTER | MEDICATED |
| TIME TO SEED | HIS COCO SP it 16990 | RUDE MONEY | THE KINGS INVENTED GRAN |
| Dr. GRIFFITH'S DIGESTIVE MIX | ZOO motive | LUNG CORD GOL | GOLD HERD |
| ED DE HOE US | ONE ANDY, ANISEED, | $E = Mc^2$ | PIGZEST |
| AIR TACLES | VODKA LIS'P 15989 | Anti-solar. City | PAPER MARS |
| TONI FIN FELATIO EFFECT | OIL MR BOND | GREAT GREATEST MOTH | EDWARDS' LIVER |
| Dr. GRIFFITH'S DIGESTIVE MIX | GO ROUND, 189 | MAN'S ORIGINAL TAPE | NURSE ATKINS SORE NIPPLE HEALER |
| A BIN MAN | THE BACON LINE | FRITH'S PILLS | LOOT ROSES NERVE |
| | | HANNAH'S ELECTRIC FLUID | QUEEN ON TOW |

## NEXT MEETING: SHOOT UP HILL

IN THE LAND OF THE BLIND THE FOUR EYED MAN IS KING.

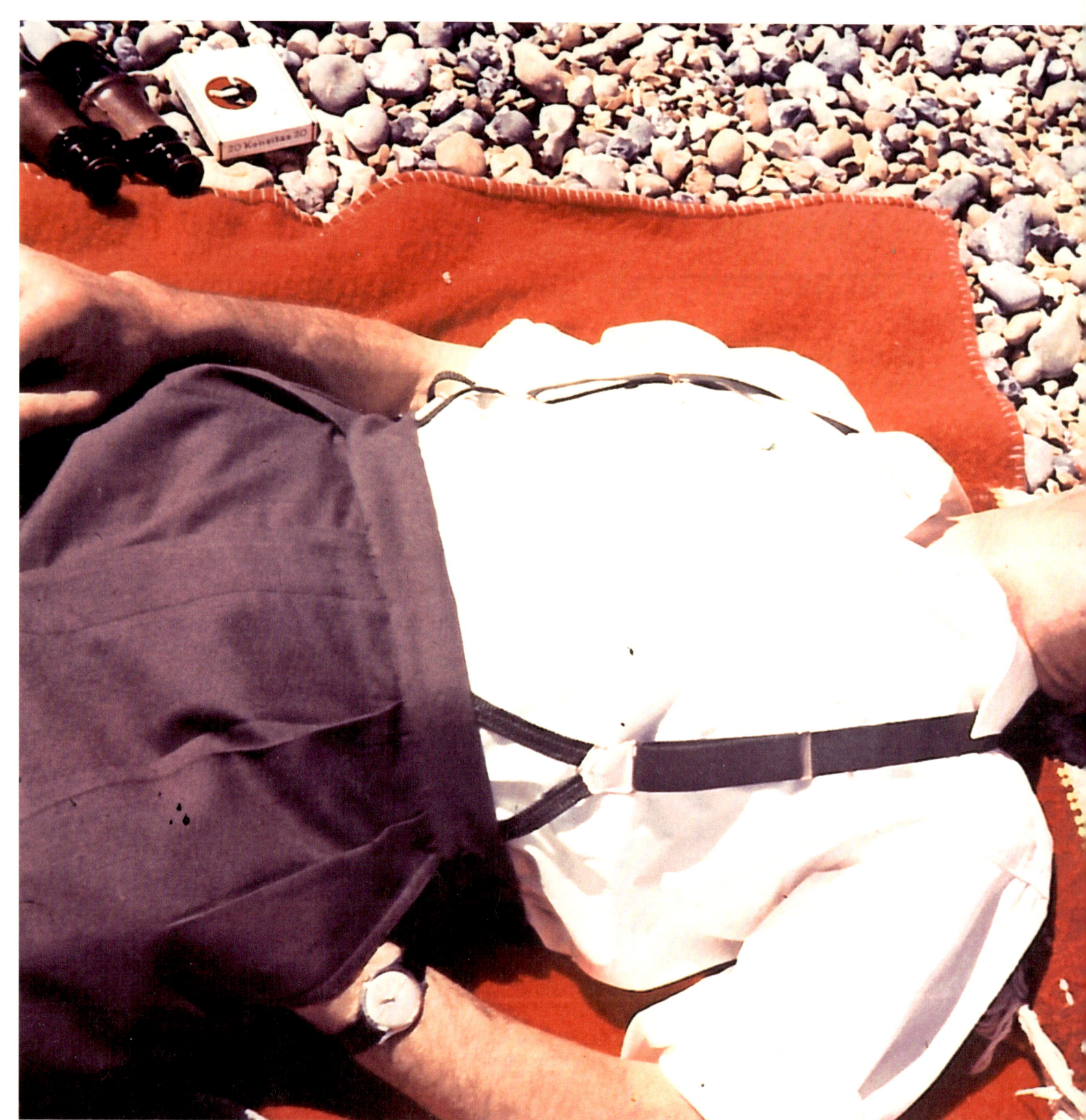

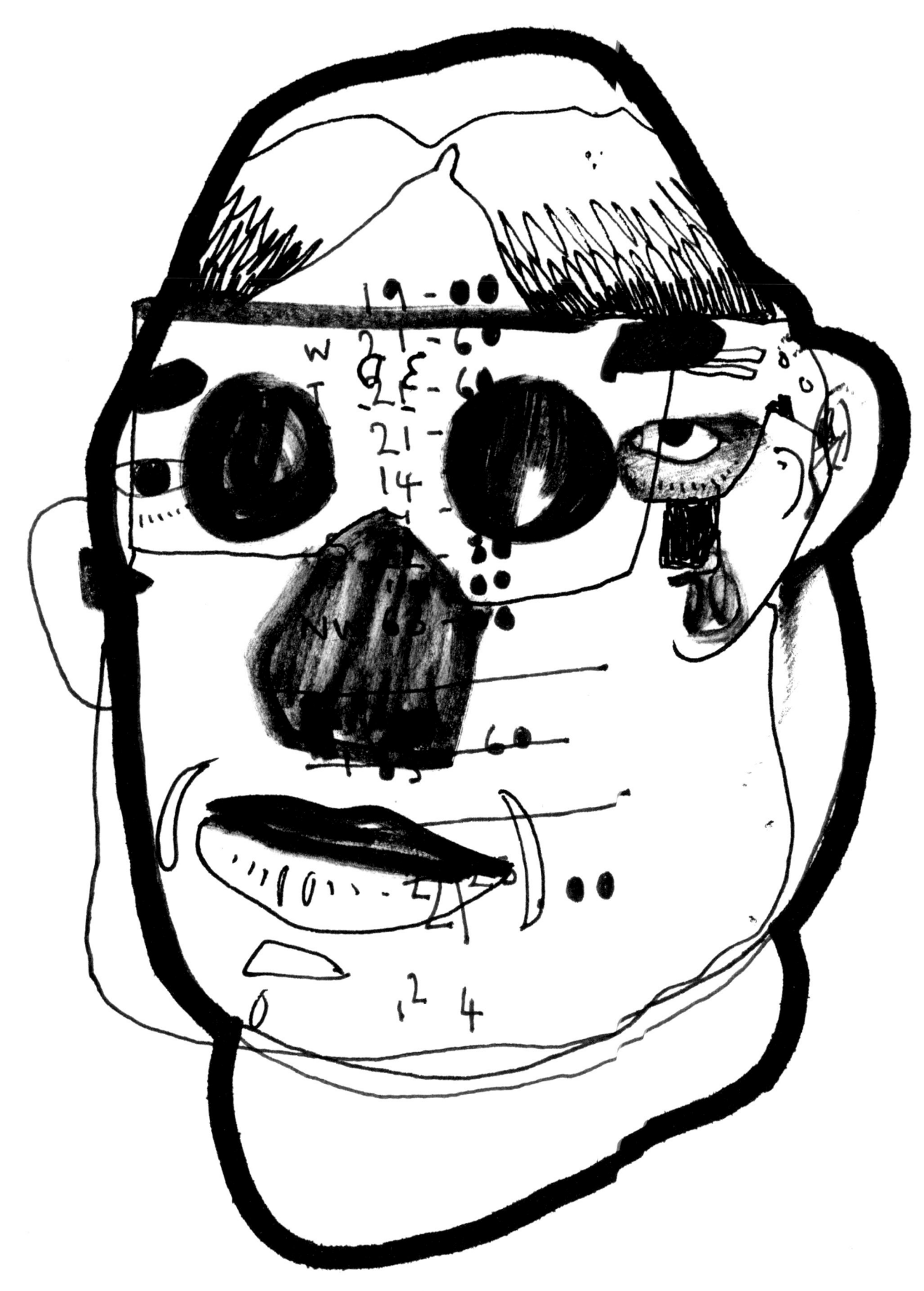

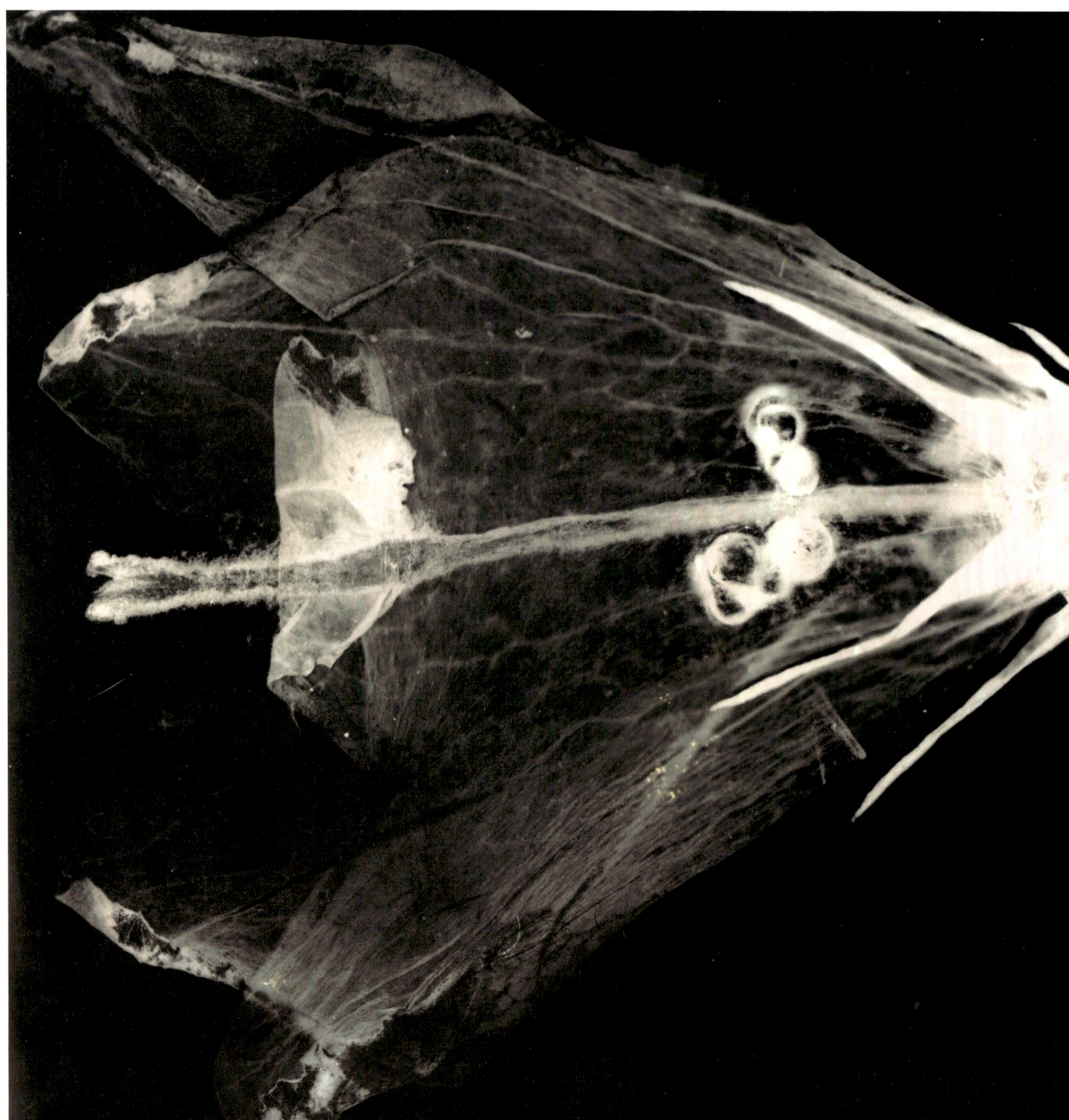

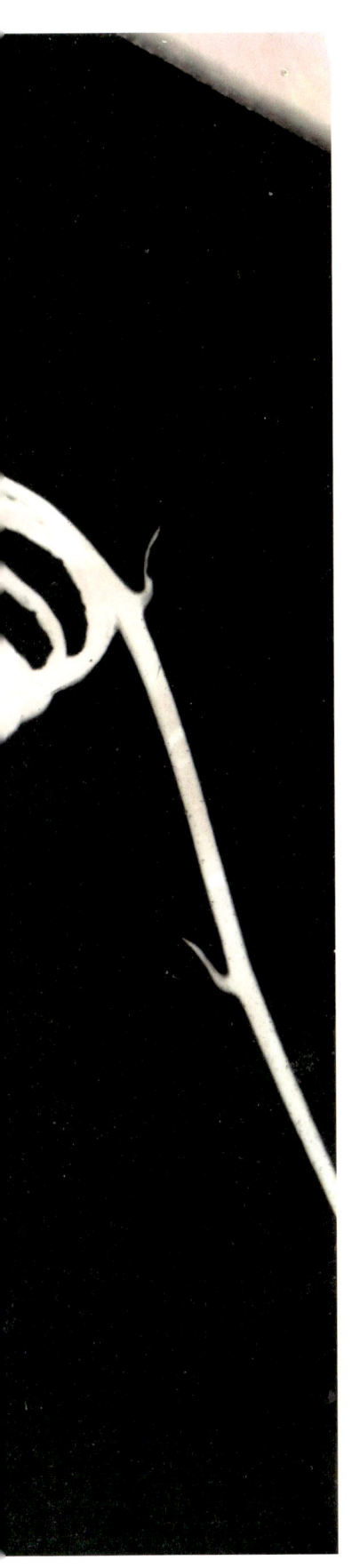

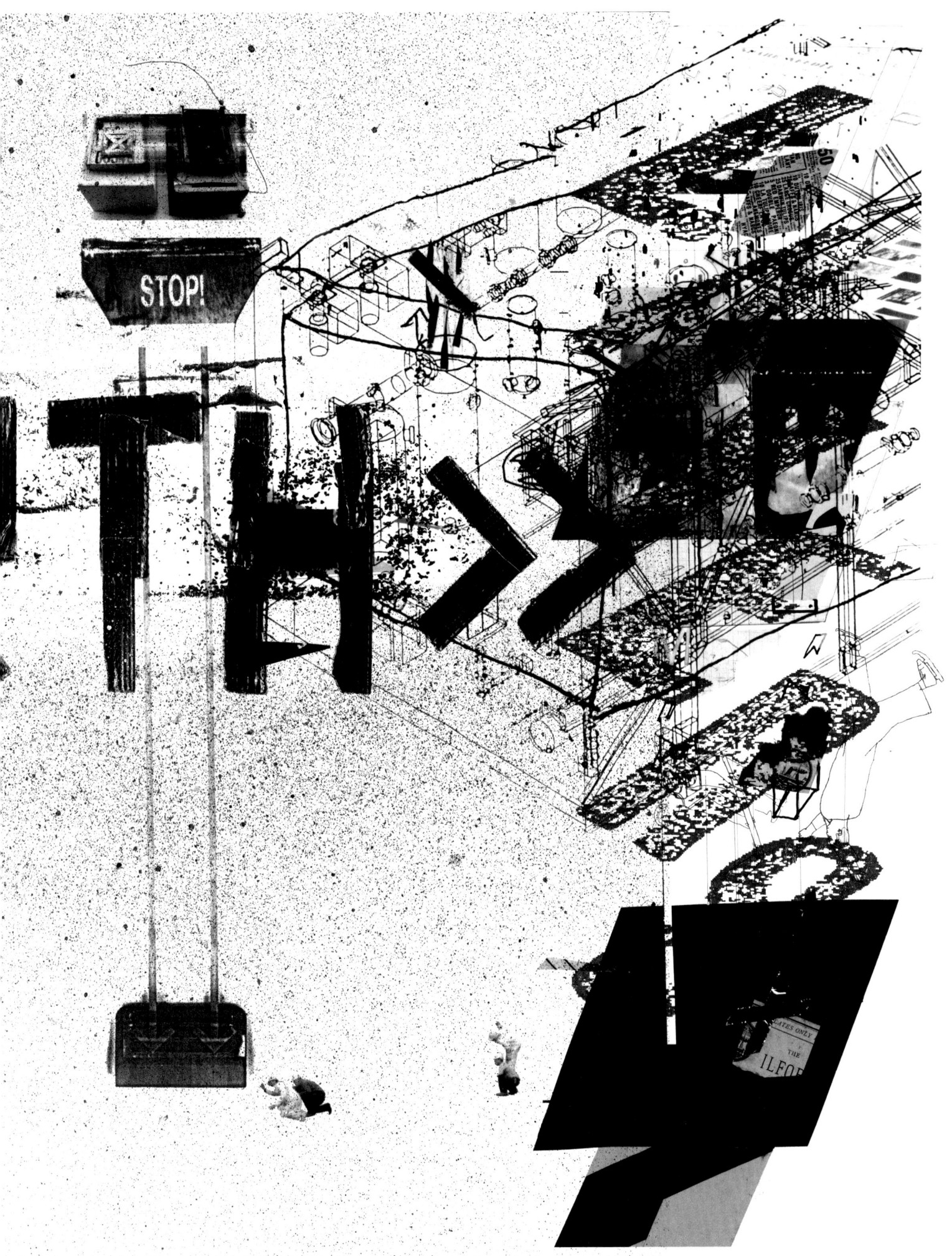

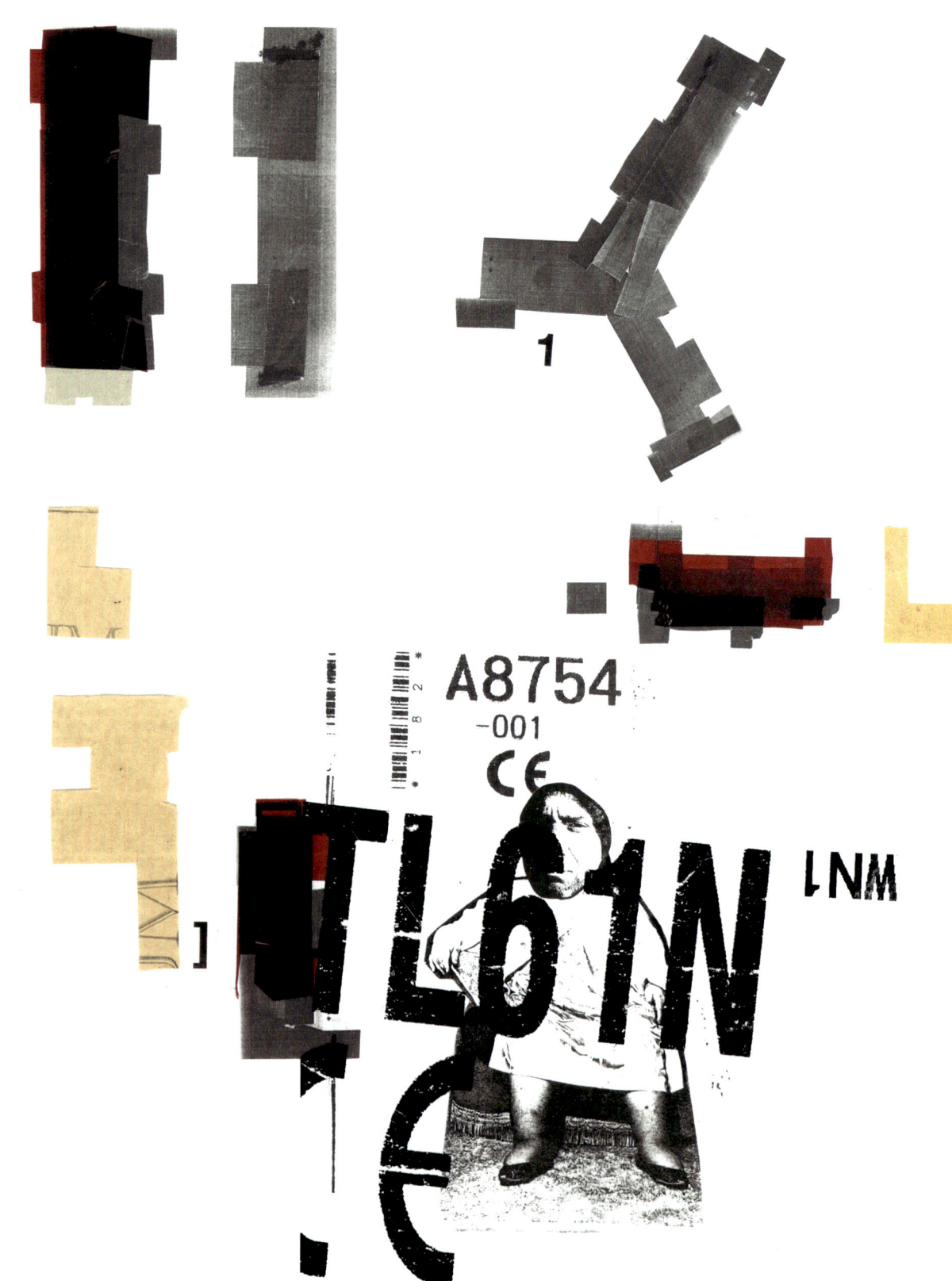

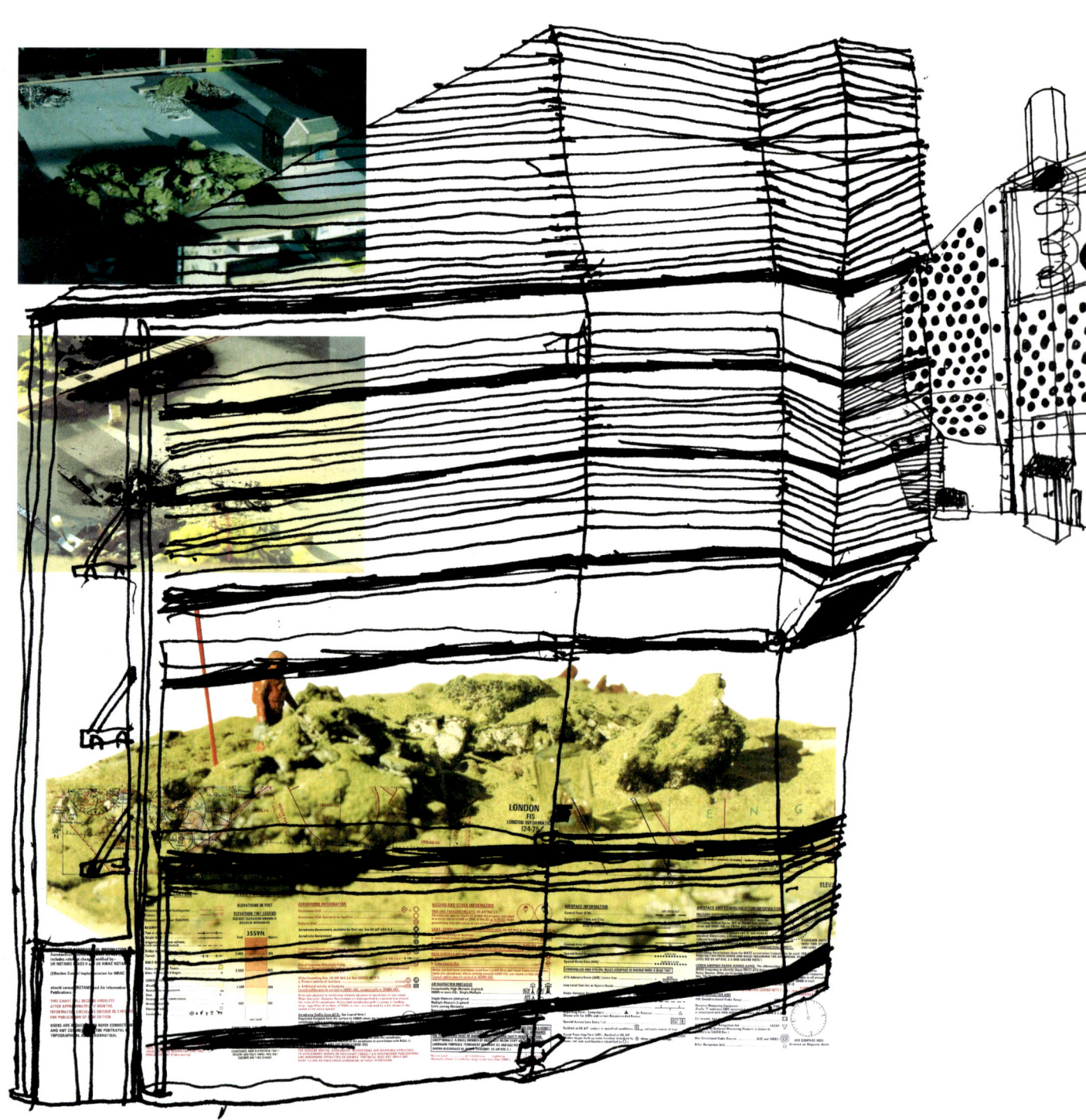

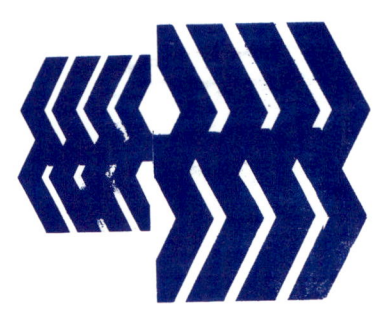
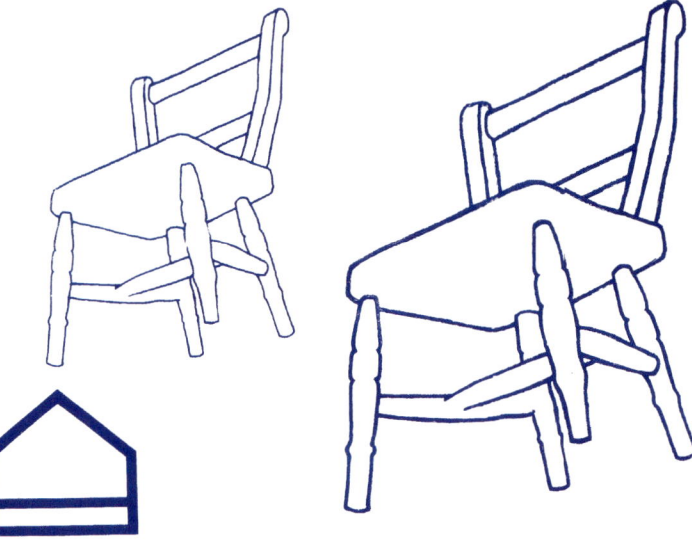

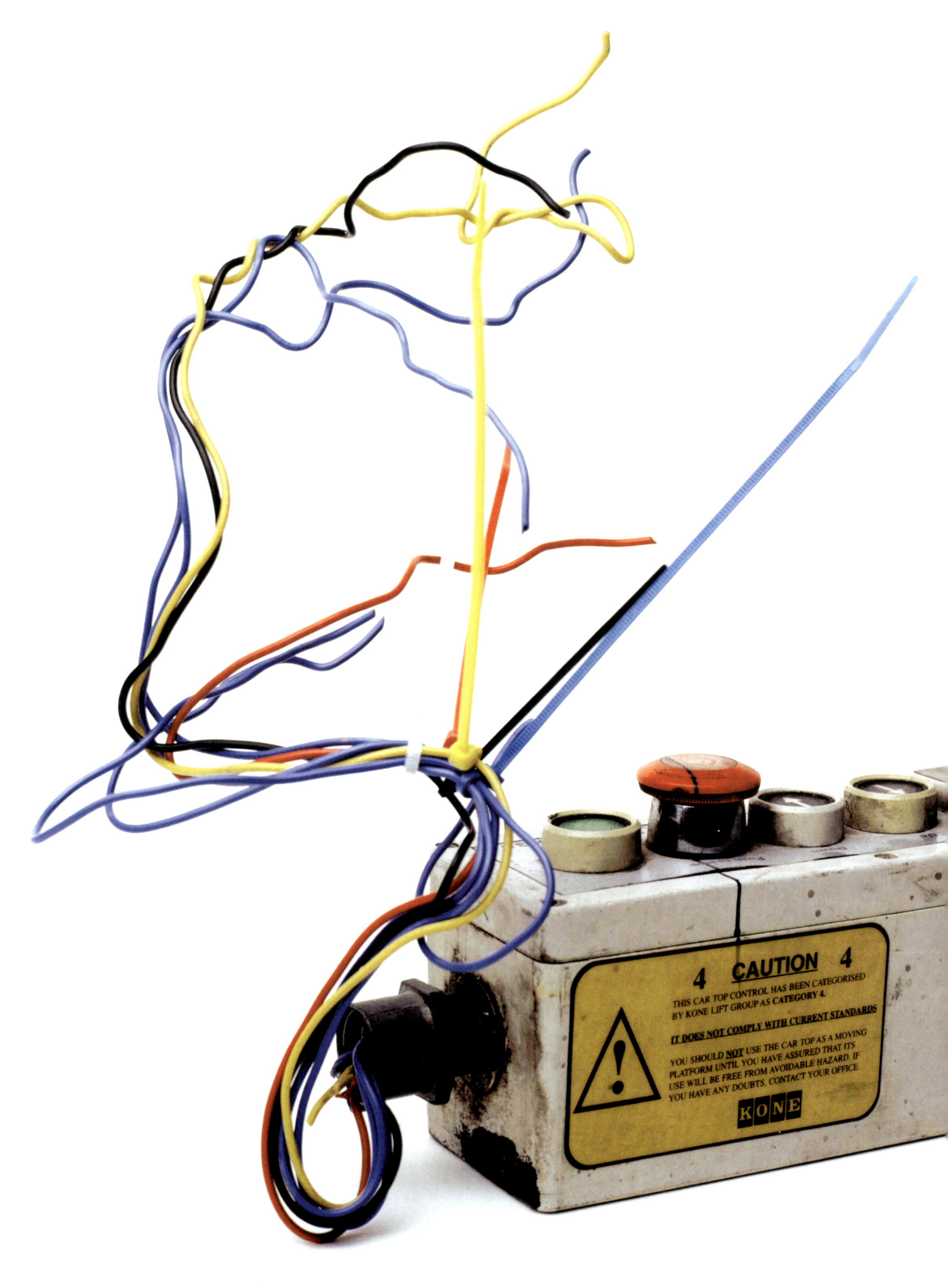

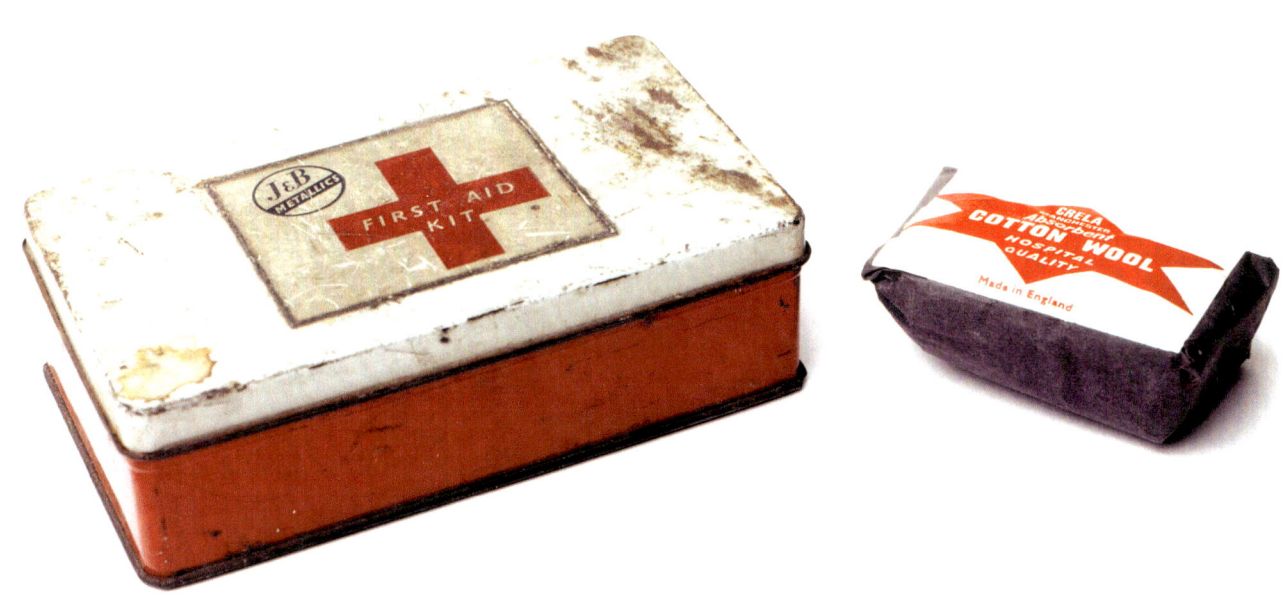

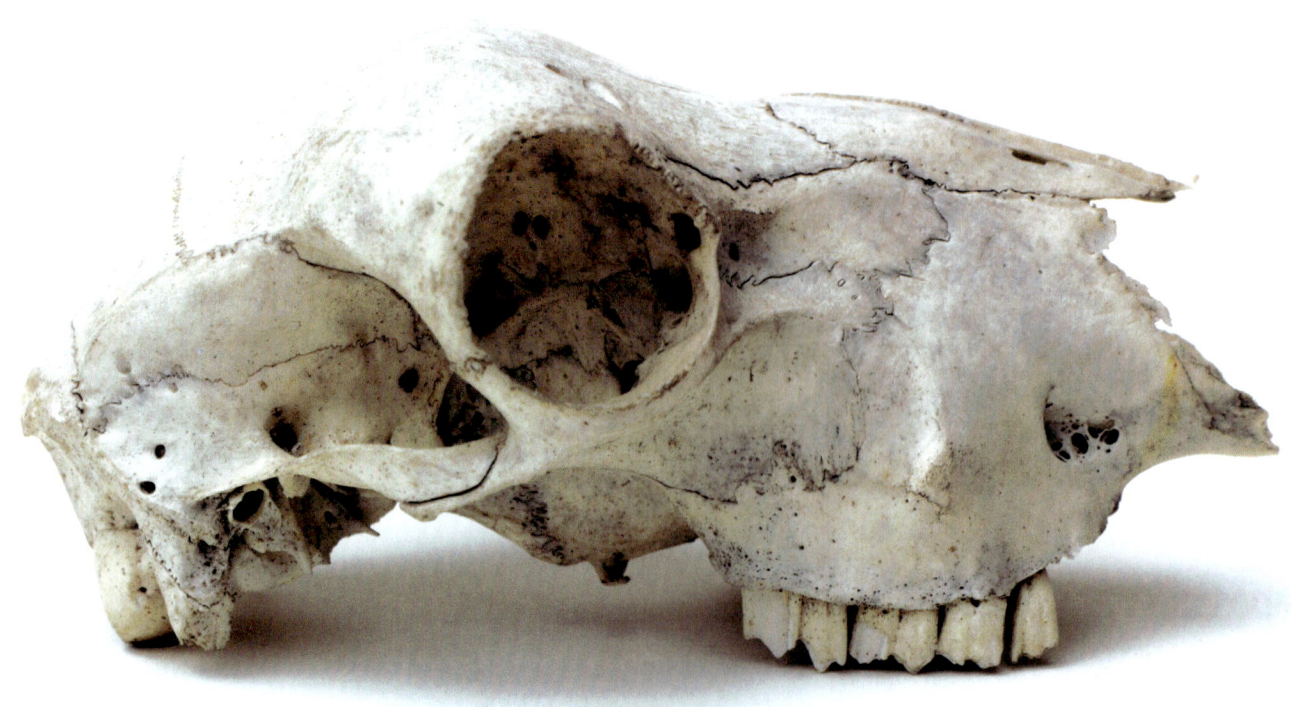

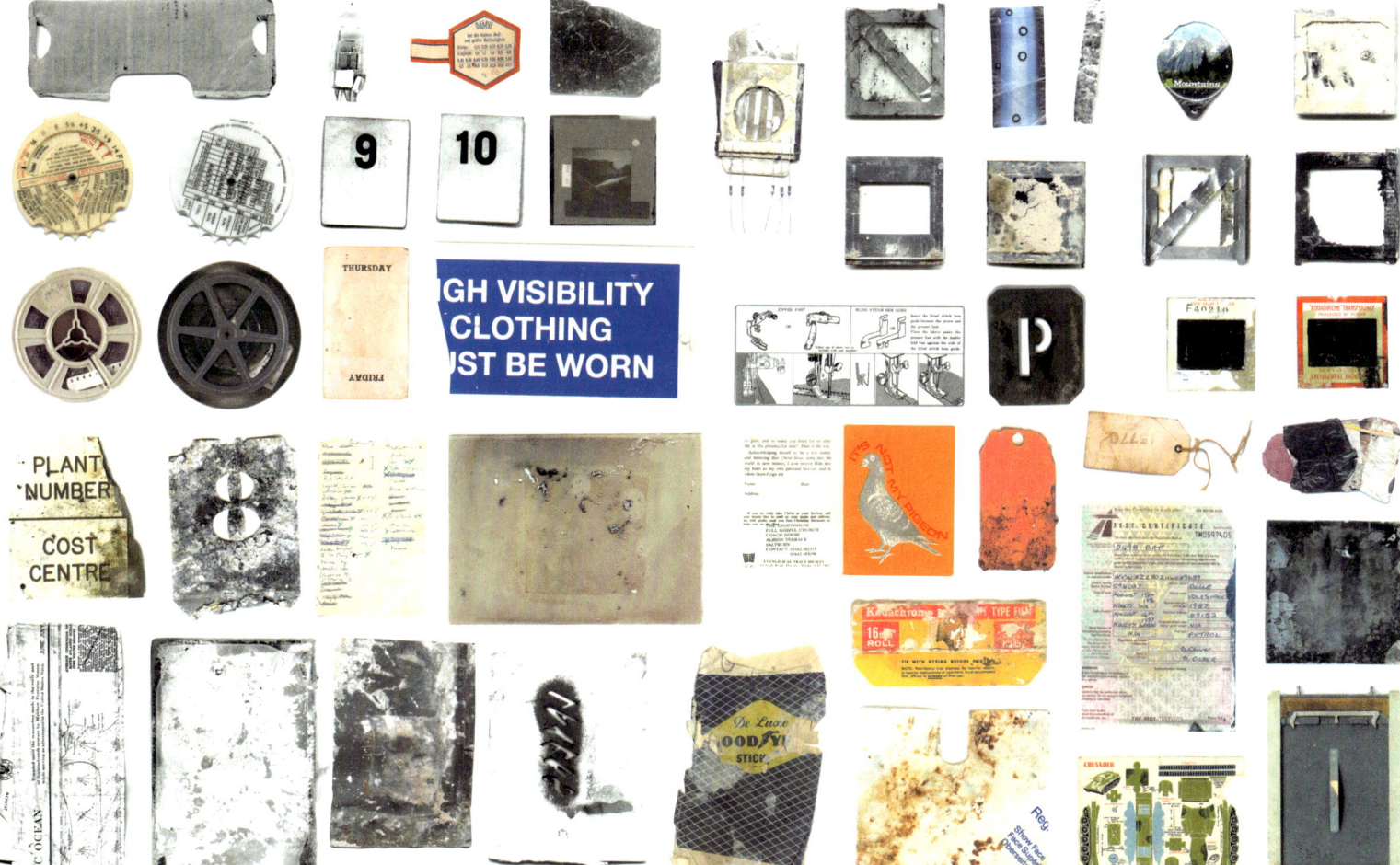

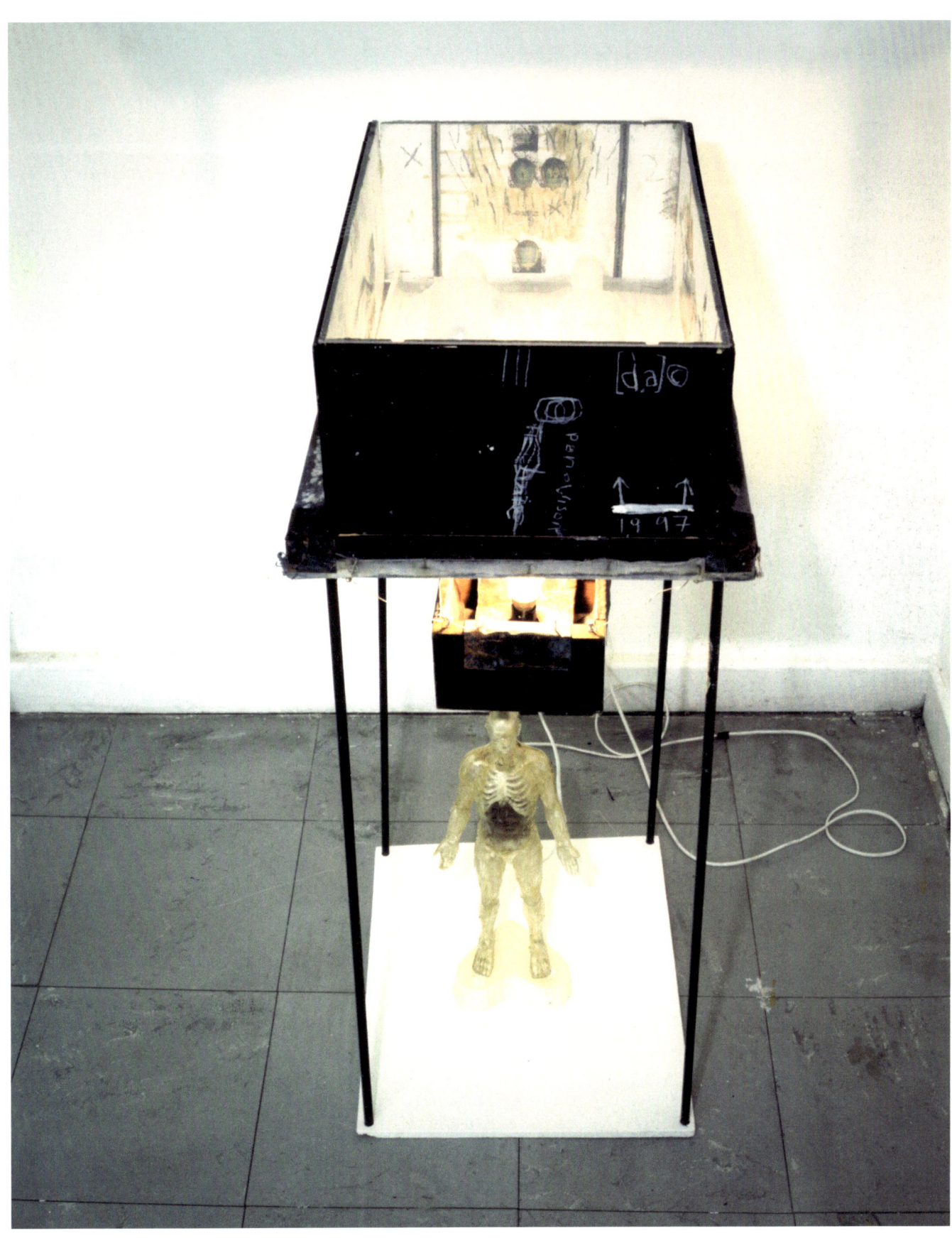

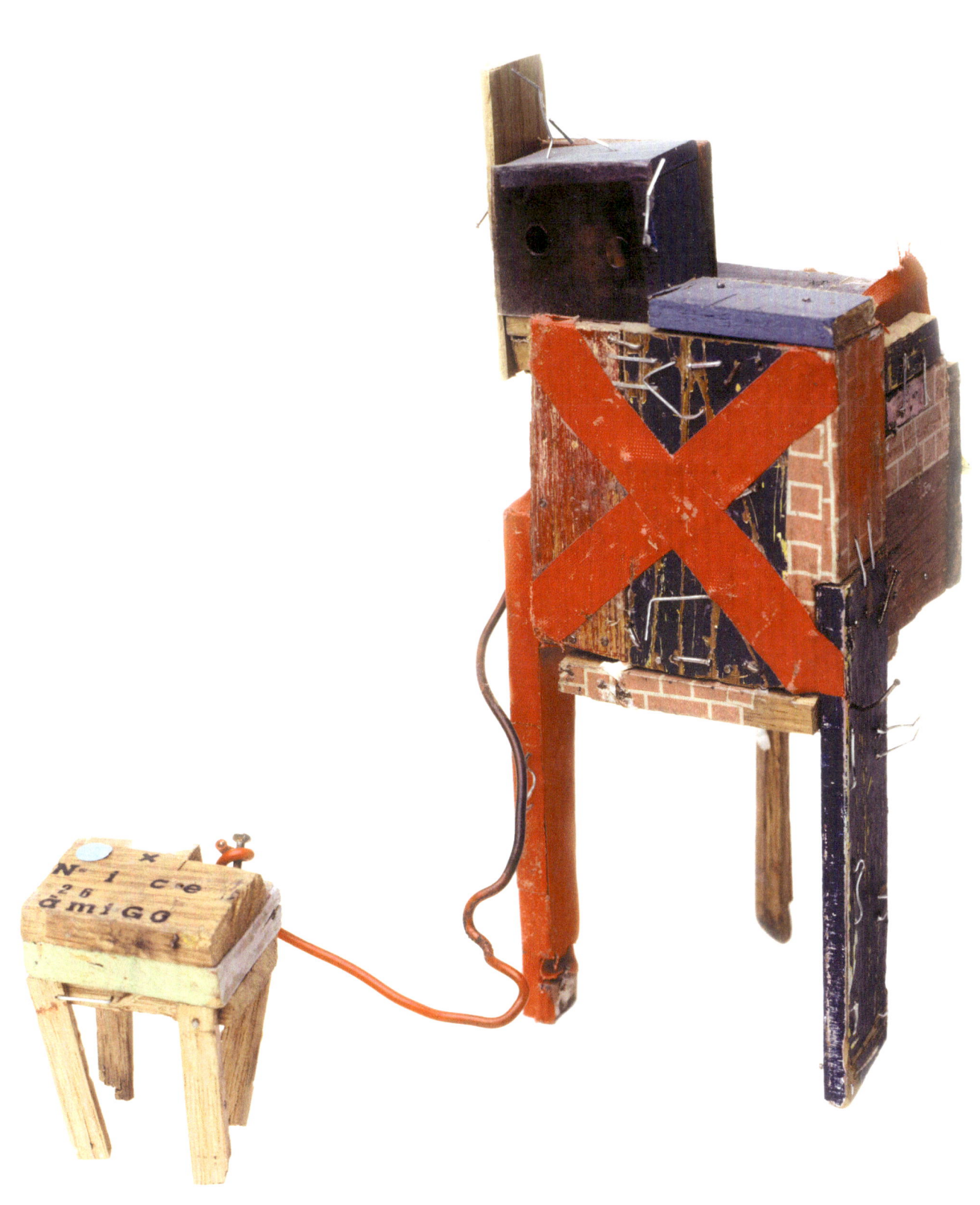

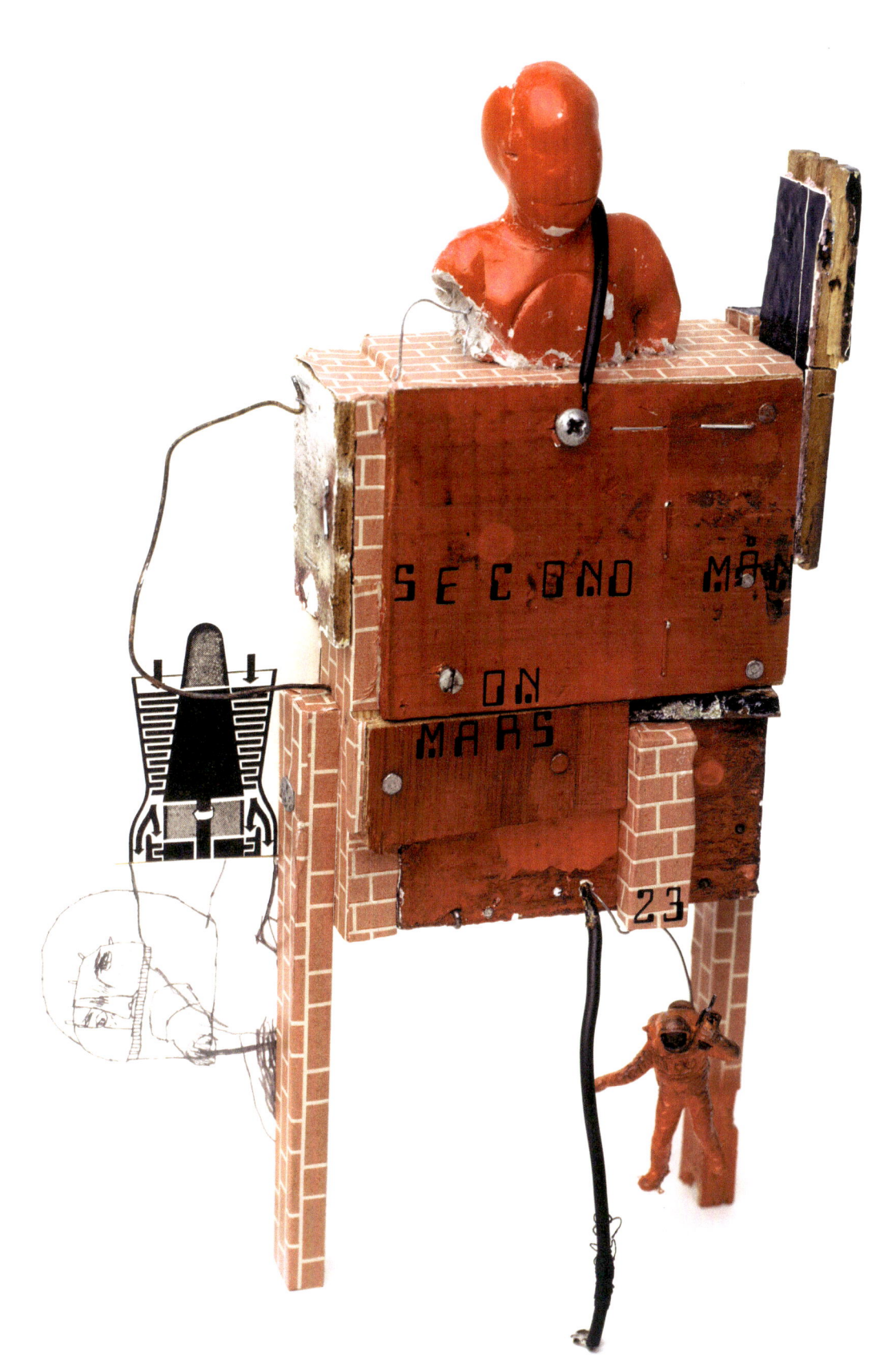

45

33

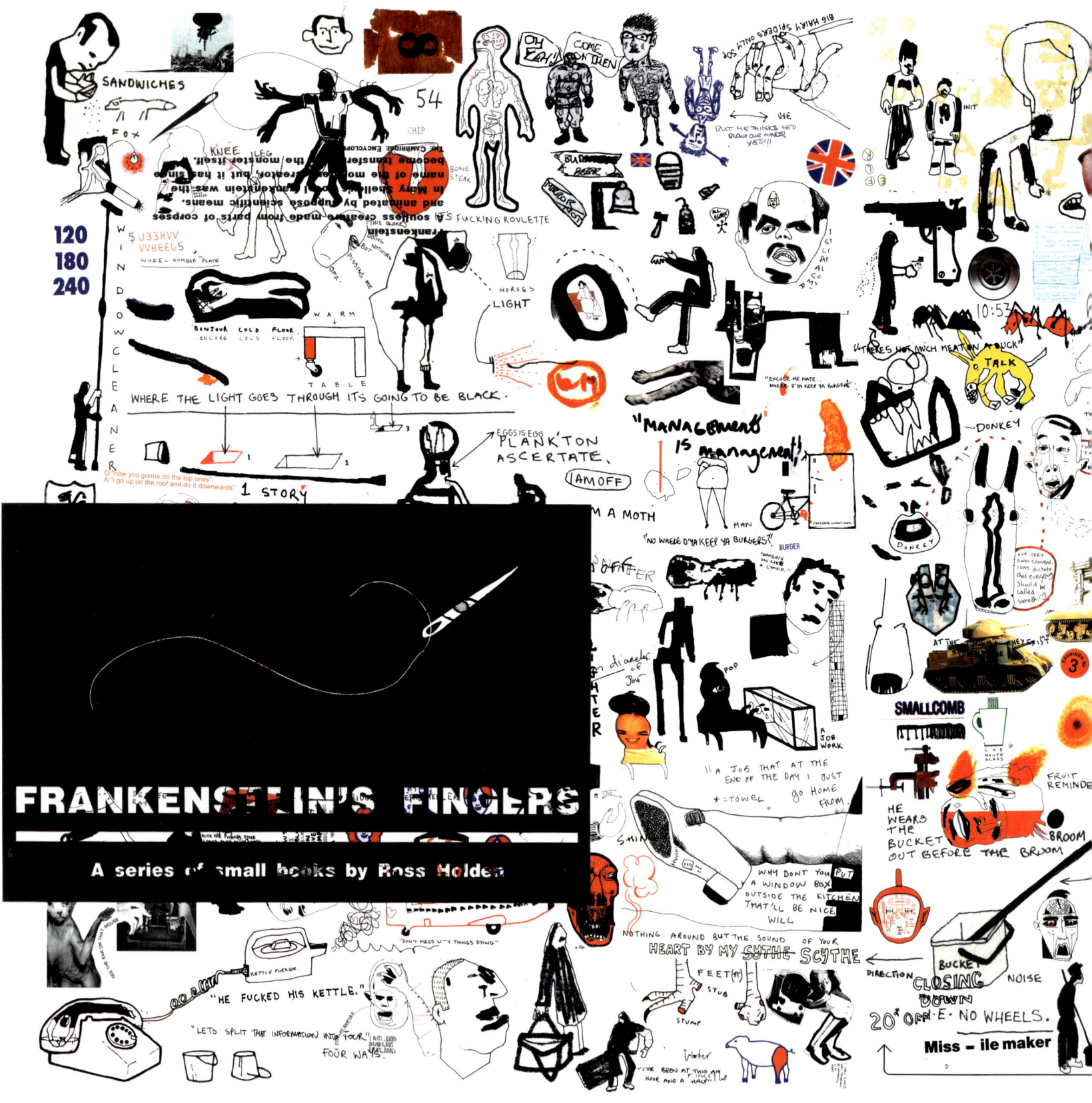

The books become like threads all coming from the s...

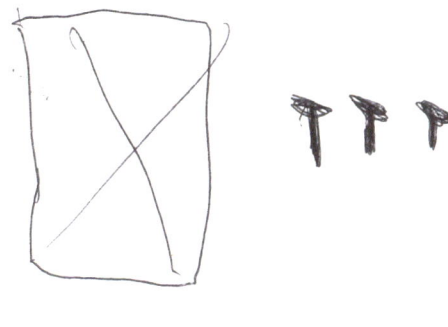

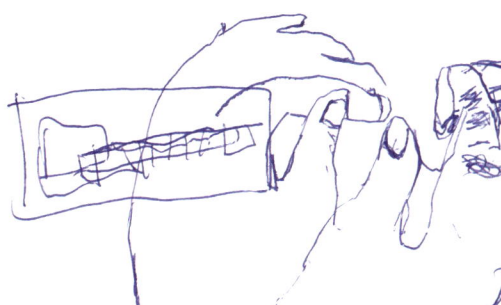

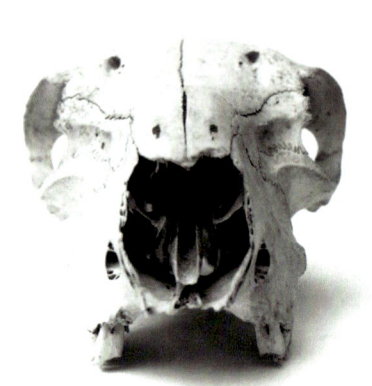

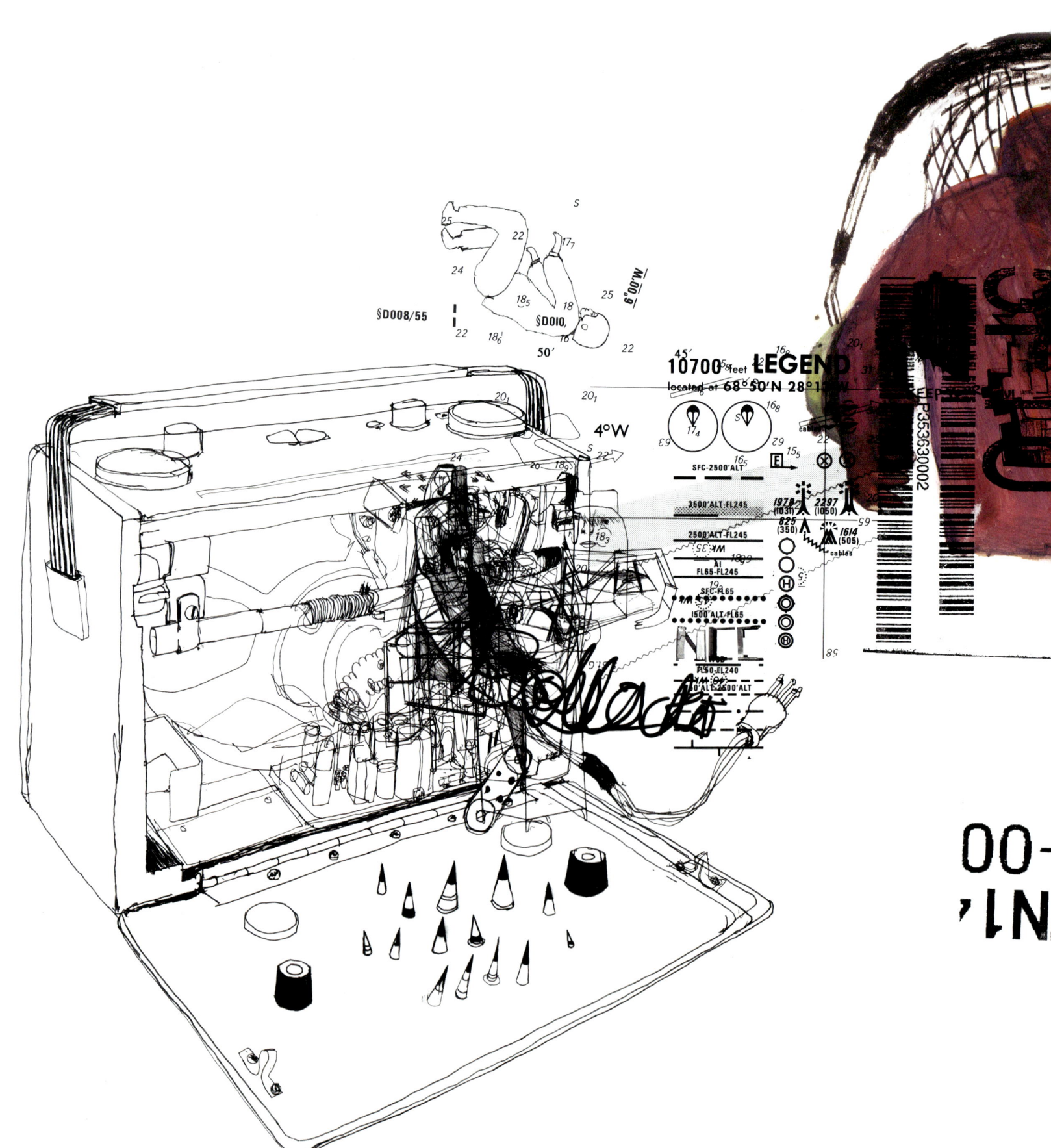

# 4th Flo

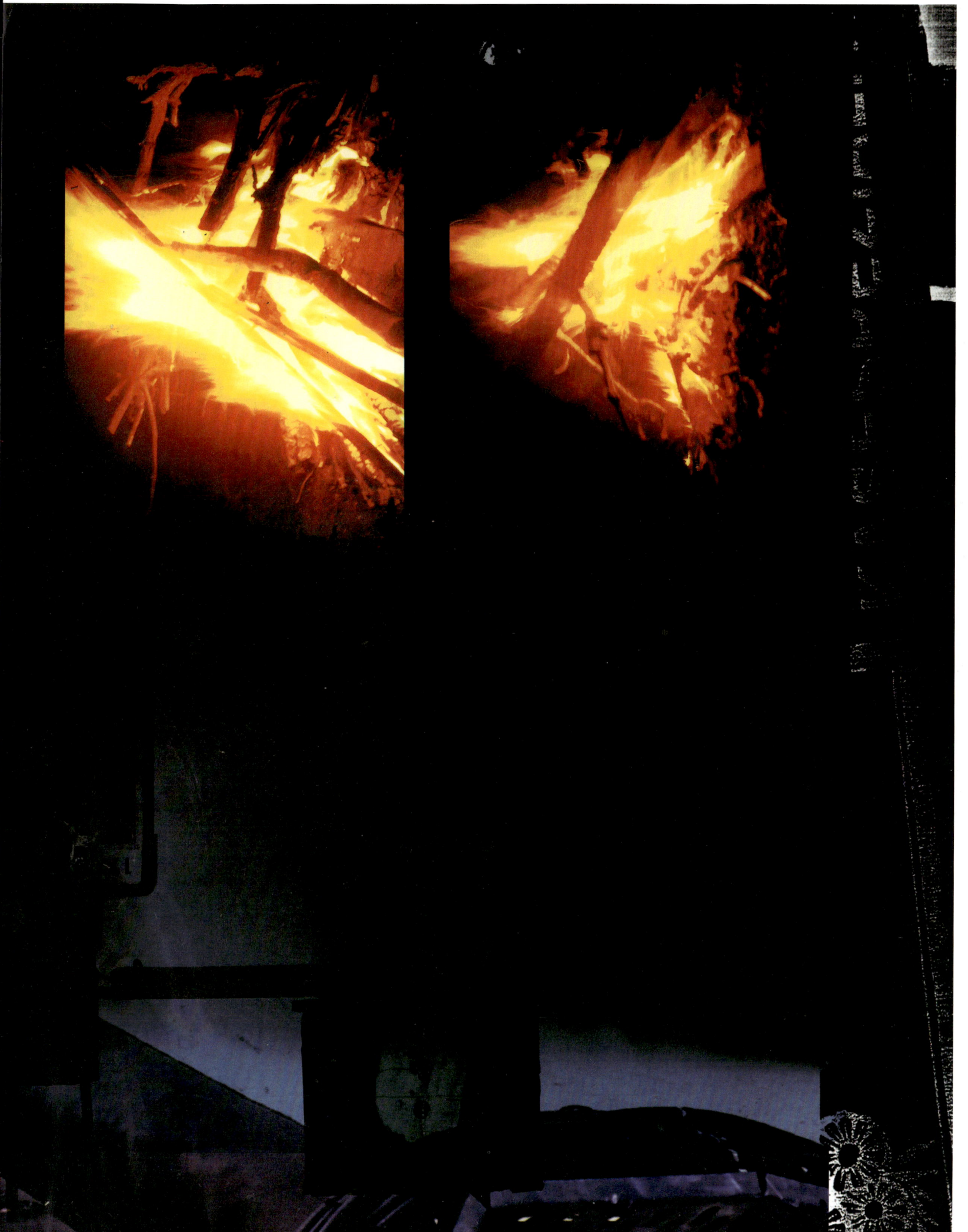

Art Center College of Design
Library
1700 Lida Street
Pasadena, Calif. 91103